This original and provocative book focusing on 'the dark side' of emotional labour weaves original research into discussions of complex debates on ethics, embodiment, capital and exploitation. It stretches the field in important and exciting directions and is essential reading for anyone with an interest in the management and experience of emotion in contemporary work organizations.

Melissa Tyler, *Professor, University of Essex, UK*

This gripping book presents an exploration of work that is at once emotionally disturbing, upsetting or stigmatising and at the same time necessary. Work that the rest of society would rather not think about. The compelling analysis leaves us under no illusion about the darker side of emotional labour even though we come to see how some people may take pride in such work.

Paula Hyde, *Professor, University of Manchester, UK*

If organizations and their members read Ward and McMurray's *The Dark Side of Emotional Labour*, working lives would change. This book brings together two decades of research on emotional labourers with a theoretically strong critique of emotional labour, a core concept in work and society and management and organization studies. This is the first rigorous take on the 'the dark side' of emotion at the level of subjectivity, care, ethics and work. A painful joy to read.

Alison Pullen, *Professor, Macquarie University, Australia*

With wisdom and clarity Jenna Ward and Robert McMurray guide us through the unfamiliar terrain of the dark side of emotional labour – emotional dirty work, emotional labour that is antipathetic, and facing abuse from customers. The authors combine a deft theoretical imagination with a close reading of rich empirical material in this beautiful and important book.

Marek Korczynski, *Professor, University of Nottingham, UK*

The Dark Side of Emotional Labour

The Dark Side of Emotional Labour explores the work that the rest of society would rather not think about, the often unseen work that is emotionally disturbing, exhausting, upsetting, and stigmatising. This is work that is simultaneously undesirable and rewarding, work whose tasks are eschewed and yet necessary for the effective function of individual organisations and society at large.

Diverse and challenging, this book examines how workers such as the doorman, the HR manager, the waiter and the doctor's receptionist experience verbal aggression and intimidation; how the prison officer and the home carer respond to the emotions associated with physical violence; and how the Samaritan, the banker and the veterinarian deal with death and despair. It also considers how different individuals develop the emotional capital necessary to cope with the dark side of emotional labour and how individuals can make sense of and come to take satisfaction and pride in such difficult work. Finally, the book considers what is to be done with darker emotional work, in terms of the management and care of those labouring on the dark side.

Challenging and original, this book gives a voice to those who undertake the most demanding work on our behalf. It will be of interest to researchers and students of organisation studies and its related fields and to every one of us who is called on to work or manage on the Dark Side.

Jenna Ward is Senior Lecturer at Leicester Business School at De Montfort University in Leicester, UK.

Robert McMurray is Senior Lecturer in Management at Durham University, UK.

Routledge Studies in Management, Organizations and Society

This series presents innovative work grounded in new realities, addressing issues crucial to an understanding of the contemporary world. This is the world of organized societies, where boundaries between formal and informal, public and private, local and global organizations have been displaced or have vanished, along with other nineteenth century dichotomies and oppositions. Management, apart from becoming a specialised profession for a growing number of people, is an everyday activity for most members of modern societies.

Similarly, at the level of enquiry, culture and technology, and literature and economics, can no longer be conceived as isolated intellectual fields; conventional canons and established mainstreams are contested. **Management, Organizations and Society** addresses these contemporary dynamics of transformation in a manner that transcends disciplinary boundaries, with books that will appeal to researchers, student and practitioners alike.

Breaking through the Glass Ceiling
Women, power and leadership in
agricultural organizations
Margaret Alston

The Poetic Logic of Administration
Styles and changes of style in the art
of organizing
Kaj Sköldberg

Casting the Other
Maintaining gender inequalities in
the workplace
*Edited by Barbara Czarniawska
and Heather Höpfl*

**Gender, Identity and the Culture of
Organizations**
*Edited by Iiris Aaltio and Albert
J. Mills*

Text/Work
Representing organization and
organizing representation
Edited by Stephen Linstead

**The Social Construction of
Management**
Texts and identities
Nancy Harding

Management Theory
A critical and reflexive reading
Nanette Monin

The Dark Side of Emotional Labour

Jenna Ward and Robert McMurray

Routledge
Taylor & Francis Group

LONDON AND NEW YORK

First published 2016
by Routledge
2 Park Square, Milton Park, Abingdon, Oxon OX14 4RN

and by Routledge
605 Third Avenue, New York, NY 10017

First issued in paperback 2020

Routledge is an imprint of the Taylor & Francis Group, an informa business

British Library Cataloguing-in-Publication Data
A catalogue record for this book is available from the British Library

Library of Congress Cataloging-in-Publication Data
Ward, Jenna.
  The dark side of emotional labour / Jenna Ward and Robert McMurray.
      pages cm. — (Routledge studies in management, organizations and society)
  Includes bibliographical references and index.
  1. Work—Psychological aspects. 2. Service industries workers—Psychology. 3. Caregivers—Psychology. 4. Organizational behavior. 5. Industrial sociology. 6. Psychology, Industrial. 7. Personnel management. I. Title.
  HF5548.8.W276 2016
  158.7—dc23
  2015016523

ISBN 13: 978-0-367-73770-2 (pbk)
ISBN 13: 978-0-415-82904-5 (hbk)

Typeset in Sabon
by Apex CoVantage, LLC

Contents

1 Introduction

'What I envy you, sir, is the luxury of your own feelings. I belong to a profession in which that luxury is sometimes denied us.'
Little Dorrit by Charles Dickens (1857[1996]:299)

'You created my job, you created me. To you, I am a robot in uniform. You press the button and when you call me to the scene you expect results. But I'm also a man. I even have a heart.'
Vincent Maher, policeman (Terkel, 1974:137)

It is more than 30 years since the publication of Hochschild's seminal book *The Managed Heart* (1983). Since then the term 'emotional labour' has become common in academic disciplines as varied as organisational studies, critical management studies, human resource management, nursing, psychology and sociology. This 'bandwagon' phenomenon (Bolton, 2005) has had the positive effect of rapidly developing the subfield of work-based studies of emotion and enriching our knowledge of emotions at work. Less welcome have been the 'semantic morass' (McClure & Murphy, 2008:105), oversights, oversimplification and myopic focus on certain sectors and certain types of emotional offering that have served to stifle the continued progression of the field (Callahan & McCollum, 2002). This is exemplified by the preoccupation with flight attendants, the symbolic 'smile' and *empathetic* emotional labour, and the relative neglect of those such as debt collectors and the *antipathetic* emotional labour (Korczynski, 2002) that characterises key aspects of their work. Both positive and negative forms of emotional labour were introduced in Hochschild's original empirical work, yet the latter, along with other, darker elements of emotional labour, remain underresearched and underdeveloped.

We take Hochschild (1983) as both starting point and referent for our focus on 'the dark side' of emotional labour. Following recent academic (e.g. Donkin, 2001; Letiche, 2009; Linstead *et al.*, 2014; McCabe, 2014) and popular interest (e.g. Vey, 2005), we explore work that the rest of society would rather not think about: work that is emotionally disturbing, wearing, deeply upsetting, stigmatising and yet necessary for the effective function of specific organisations and society at large (McMurray & Ward, 2014). In so doing we draw on examples from our own research across the public, private and voluntary sectors to analyse the experiences of bankers, nurses, veterinarians, receptionists, police officers, airline staff, home care workers, Samaritans, directors of human resources, prison officers, door staff, school teachers and hotel workers. By including such a broad range of individuals we not only widen the fairly narrow empirical focus of the emotional labour fieldwork to date but also attend to Hughes's (1984) call to look for those factors that both separate and cut across different occupations whether they be humble or proud. To this end we explore how workers as diverse as the bouncer, the HR manager, the waiter and the doctor's receptionist experience verbal aggression and intimidation; how the prison officer and the home carer respond to the emotions associated with physical violence; and how the Samaritan, the banker and the veterinarian deal with death and despair. We also consider how different individuals develop the emotional capital necessary to cope with the darker side of emotional labour and how occupational members make sense of and come to take satisfaction and pride in such difficult work.

We begin this chapter with a brief overview of some of the emergent literature on the 'dark side' of organisations, paying particular attention to the ways in which the metaphor has been used in mainstream and more critical bodies of literature. In acknowledging the variety of appreciations and perspectives of what might constitute the 'dark side' of organisational practices, process and experiences, we turn to focus on their applicability to the emotional labour thesis specifically. The popularity of the emotional labour construct has led to it being studied in more subject areas than we could name, but they include sociology, psychology, nursing studies, pedagogy and social psychology. It is perhaps unsurprising, then, that there are potentially many 'dark sides' of emotional labour that have been commented on. In presenting a cross-disciplinary review of the extant literature, we briefly map out four more well-rehearsed critiques which throw the emotional labour construct in what could be argued to be 'the darkness'. Specifically, we discuss 'darkness' in relation to emotional labour discourse as *exploitation*, as *alienation*, as *dissonance* and as *gendered accounts*. In so doing, we seek to highlight a very different appreciation of the 'dark side of emotional labour', one that is experientially uncomfortable, challenging, unspoken and even hidden. From this alternative vantage point, we get to hear the lived experiences, the pain, the joy and the indifference associated with undertaking work that the rest of society would rather not know much about. This text, then, seeks to move the debate on through a combination of our own empirical research and existing studies to demonstrate the complexity and prevalence of emotion management that is being carried out in various work contexts. Moreover, we consider what is to be done with darker emotional work, in terms of both the management of such work and the care of workers labouring on the dark side of emotional labour.

The 'dark side'

The 'dark side' metaphor emerged most visibly in the 1990s as a critical response to frustrations with mainstream managerialism's reluctance to address difficult ethical, political and ideological issues that arise within and from organisational practices, process and experiences (*Linstead et al.*, 2014). Over time, interest in the 'dark side' of organisations has grown, and the field has attracted a range of scholars who self-identify an interest in the exploration and understanding of the phenomenon. It is now generally accepted that there is a dark, negative or asocial side to organisations (Linstead *et al.*, 2014; Banjeree & Linstead, 2001; Klein, 2007; Vaughan, 1999; Griffin & O'Leary-Kelly, 2004). However, what constitutes darkness, why it occurs and with what consequences are issues that serve to identify emerging tropes in the way the 'dark side' of organisations is conceptualised and understood.

Mainstream approaches characterise the 'dark side' of organisations as incidents, experiences or behaviours that are perceived to be 'abnormal, by-product(s) of dysfunctional relations (McCabe, 2014:255). Here, then, the 'dark side' is itself abnormal and dysfunctional in that it runs counter to managerialist ideologies of control. For Vaughan the study of the dark side is 'how things go wrong in socially organized settings' (1999:273), usually as a consequence of mistakes, misconduct and disasters. In the managerial, functional literature, these incidents are attributed to a lack of conformity and ineffective leadership, resulting in deviations from the formal design, goals and standards of the organisational context (Vaughan, 1999). In this regard, 'better organisational performance', more 'effective management' and more 'compliant employees' would eradicate the 'dark side'.

Muhr and Rehn (2014) complicate the simplicity of such functionalist arguments, however, by demonstrating that organisations can utilise and have utilised organisational atrocities for their own gain, despite having no part in their making – something they refer to as 'managing the external dark side as a productive resource in the form of brand image'. In their article they use the Body Shop's capitalisation on international atrocities against women to build a positive, antithetic brand identity as an example of these types of behaviours.

More critical approaches to the study of the 'dark side' offer a more complex understanding of what might constitute 'dark' organisational behaviours, choices and experiences within workplace settings from a variety of perspectives. Despite the diversity of approaches and conceptualisations of 'darkness' from critical scholars, there is an assumption that most share: the dark side is a 'condition or consequence of the normal, functional dynamics of how organisations operate in a capitalist system' (McCabe, 2014:255).

Consequently, rather than perceiving, researching and conceptualising the 'dark side' as abnormal, dysfunctional and something to be eradicated, this body of work embraces it as a lived reality of contemporary organisational life. Perhaps the most dominant critical view of the 'dark side' is that which takes issue with the 'incipient totalitarianism' (Willmott, 1993:515) of the capitalist labour process, in which managerial control has continued to extend beyond the physical labour process to include individual subjectivity. Here, then, total quality management, business process re-engineering and normative and neo-normative controls (Fleming, 2013) could all be attributed to the dark side as they seek to colonise employee subjectivity as a resource to be manipulated for organisational benefit.

Of course, emotional labour fits neatly into this analysis, for Hochschild (1983) makes it very clear that her observations were of an extension of managerial control beyond physical labour to that which was once a private part of the self – individual emotion. These types of (ethical) concerns are the focus of labour process analyses of emotional labour in which 'darkness' is exploitation and alienation. So too are the psychological consequences of performing emotions that are inauthentic to a 'real feeling'. In this latter sense, 'darkness' is presented in the literature in terms of dissonance. Finally, work that involves 'emotion' has been positioned as 'women's work', which has cast a long, dark shadow over the study and practice of emotional labour; hence, we argue that gendered accounts of emotional labour can also be read as a form of 'darkness'. We briefly introduced these well-rehearsed critiques later; however, our interpretation of the 'dark side of emotional labour' is one that is more aligned to McCabe's (2014:258) appreciation of the 'dark side' organisation in that it 'should not simply be equated with the violation of corporate rules but may indeed result from conformity with them and so actions must be assessed against their human costs'. Consequently, our study focuses on what McCabe (2014) would call 'victims of the dark side', but victims who are able to talk to the ways in which they can they take pride and satisfaction in difficult, dirty and disconcerting emotional work that most of us would rather not acknowledge has to be done. In this way, we do not construct all emotional labourers as victims; rather, we give voice to the multiplicity and complexity of the work they do and how they feel about it.

Darkness as exploitation

Hochschild (1975, 1979, 1983, 1989) presents emotional labour as the rational commodification of what was once seen, and perhaps should be, a private part of our selves: our feelings and emotions. Presenting work-based narratives from both airborne cabin crew and land-based debt collectors, Hochschild demonstrated ways in which the terms 'physical' and 'mental' labour did not adequately describe the work undertaken in these job roles. She convincingly presented the argument that employee emotions had become subject to managerial remote control, that both the men and women she interviewed and observed were, in effect, selling an emotional part of their selves to their employing organisations in exchange for a wage. She accordingly deployed the term 'emotional labour' to designate:

> the management of feeling to create a publicly observable facial and bodily display; emotional labour is sold for a wage and therefore has *exchange-value*. . . This labour requires one to induce or suppress feeling in order to sustain the outward countenance that produces the proper state of mind in others.
>
> (Hochschild, 1983:7, emphasis in original)

As a sociologist, Hochschild self-identified the origin of her thoughts on emotional labour in her reading of Marx. Though this has been disputed (e.g. Brook, 2009; Bolton, 2009) she herself contends that organisations commodify individuals' emotions in return for a wage to the extent that particular emotions come to have 'exchange value'. This process of commodification is seen by Hochschild to be in line with Marx's depiction of the labour process as exploitative in terms of the capitalist extraction and accumulation of surplus value. This perceived economic exploitation was compounded, for Hochschild, by fear that employer control over formally private parts of the self could have negative psychological and physiological consequences for the worker. In this sense, emotional labour's 'dark side' came in the form of economic, political, health and moral concerns.

Hochschild's book (1983) was intended to act as the opening rather than the concluding statement on emotional labour. She was aware of the potential limitations of her carefully selected empirical samples of flight attendant and bill collectors. For this reason she encouraged further research into the effects and varieties of emotional labour by modestly suggesting that *The Managed Heart* aimed only to 'introduce the concept of "emotional labour" and "feeling rules" (the norms which govern emotional labour), and the "emotional exchanges" on which these bear' (Hochschild, 1989:441). Over the next 30 years the challenge of better understanding emotions at work was taken up across a range of disciplines in a variety of different ways.

Darkness as alienation

Neofunctionalists were energised by the concept of feeling rules, emphasising the rule-governed aspect of micro-interactions to elucidate the multidimensional nature of service interactions. Human capital economists warmed to the transactional approach toward emotions, while labour process researchers saw it as an extension to the new vocabularies of (de-)skilling, control and resistance that they had been developing post-Braverman (1974). Yet much of this work interpreted the emotional labour thesis pessimistically (Wouters, 1989a,b). Accordingly, between 1983 and 1989 both the psychological and the sociological literature focused attention on the negative consequences of performing emotional labour in very narrow terms. Burnout, emotional exhaustion, alienation, depersonalisation, stress, depression and self-estrangement were all offered as potential consequences of emotional labour (Hochschild, 1983; Ashforth & Humphrey, 1993; Ashforth & Tomiuk, 2000). The commodification of private emotions and sentiments was argued to leave the emotional labourer with an unstable self-identity, unsure of who they were, '*estranged or alienated from an aspect of self*' (Hochschild, 1983:7). Much but not all of the psychological literature on emotional labour still retains this focus, establishing relationships between the performance of (different types of) emotional labour and its (various) consequences for subjective well-being, job satisfaction and even physical health (Bolton, 2010:207–8; Holman *et al.*, 2008; Mesmer-Magnus *et al.*, 2012).

For Wouters (1989a) the cause of these narrow concerns is to be laid at Hochschild's feet insofar as the 'preoccupation with the "costs" of emotion management not only leads to a one-sided and moralistic interpretation of the working conditions of flight attendants, it also hampers understanding the joy the job may bring' (1989a:116). In response, Hochschild argued that her drawing on Marx was to focus attention on the changing nature or quality of the constraints on workers, rather than on the quantity of those constraints and their associated outcomes. Social constraints upon workers were, she argued, increasingly aimed at an individual internal level as 'we are controlled to a greater extent through our feelings, and less through our externally observable behaviour' (Hochschild, 1989:442). The Hochschild and Wouters debate (Wouters, 1989a,b; Hochschild, 1989) arguably marked the point of departure between sociology's and psychology's treatment of emotional labour as much of the sociological literature began to reconsider the effects of emotional labour and came to focus instead on identifying job roles that required the management of emotion. What Hochschild's work does highlight in sociological terms is the need to understand such work-based performances as inherently complex emotional interactions that shape and are shaped by our approach to organising. Psychology, as well as other more positivistically driven disciplines, continued to pursue evidence of causal relationships between emotional labour performances and their impact on job satisfaction and individual well-being, with considerable attention being afforded to the mitigating role of emotional dissonance.

Darkness as dissonance

Morris and Feldman (1996) take a functionalist view of the dimensions, antecedents and consequences of emotional labour, concluding that *only* emotional dissonance leads to lower job satisfaction. They epigrammatically asserted that emotional dissonance is caused by 'having to express organisationally desired emotions not genuinely felt' (Morris & Feldman, 1996:986). This spoke to the negative effect of role conflict and to the danger that performance of multiple (potentially conflicting) 'social roles' could foster feelings of inauthenticity. Emotional labour here was not considered to be a negative concept (a side effect of capitalism) but was depoliticised as a multidimensional construct. Perhaps confusingly, psychology does not use the term 'emotional labour' but prefers the designation 'emotion work'; the latter shows little regard for public-private context or exchange/use-value, being interested only in individual behaviour and intrapsychic processes (Zapf, 2002). This is justified on the basis that Hochschild claimed that the act of regulation is the same both inside and outside the work context.

Psychological studies, then, attempted to refine Morris and Feldman's conceptualisation of dissonance and its relationship with other work-related factors, such as satisfaction and commitment, control and resistance (although these latter terms were not politicised in the same ways as they were in sociology). Abraham (1998, 1999, 2000) defined 'emotional dissonance' as the 'conflict between experienced emotions and emotions expressed to conform to display rules' (Abraham, 1999:441) and found that emotional dissonance, as a result of imposed conformity, led to job dissatisfaction, which subsequently had a negative impact on organisational commitment and labour turnover (Abraham, 1999). This relationship was found to be more acute in individuals with highly developed 'self-monitoring capabilities' who were more reflexively aware of their dissonant feelings. Abraham (1999), like Morris and Feldman (1996), suggests this is a result of role conflict and, thus, theorises emotional dissonance to be a state in which core values are compromised by required emotional displays; this 'represents such a fundamental attack on the self that . . . alienation and hostility [are] aroused' (1999:451). However, in an earlier study (1998) she reported that the relationship between emotional dissonance and job dissatisfaction was mediated by social support from coworkers, with social support preventing job dissatisfaction from occurring at all.

It is important to recognise that Abraham's (1998, 1999, 2000) work, along with that of Morris and Feldman (1996), makes the implicit assumption that *emotional dissonance is a product of emotional labour*. This is not an assumption shared by researchers in all disciplines. Van Dijk and Kirk-Brown's (2006) quantitative study argues that the consequences of performing emotional labour are *mediated by* emotional dissonance in that 'emotional dissonance is not necessarily an automatic outcome of performing emotional labour when felt and displayed emotions are incongruent' (Van Dijk & Kirk-Brown, 2006:113). A more recent large scale meta-analysis conducted by Mesmer-Magnus *et al.* (2012:6) builds on the idea of (in) congruence in presenting an emotional labour framework 'wherein various aspects of emotional labour are understood through the underlying *discordance* versus *congruence* in felt versus displayed emotions' (emphasis in original). Collating 109 independent studies on emotional labour, they identified a recurring pattern that suggests 'discordant' forms of emotional labour (e.g. surface acting and emotional dissonance) are associated with darker experiences and consequences such as burnout, emotional exhaustion and stress.

Despite Mesmer-Magnus *et al.*'s (2012) attempts to draw out a unified set of findings from existing studies, their sample consists of empirical studies that are broadly from psychology. Haywood and Tuckey (2011:1503) see this disciplinary focus as part of the problem with emotional labour research, arguing that 'there remains a need to go beyond these diverse operational definitions of emotion work to get to the heart of emotion management'. Similarly, Wharton (2009) argues that emotional labour scholars should pay more attention to social-psychological theories of emotion to help further our understanding of emotional labour, whilst in a similar vein Scott and Barnes (2011:132) call for more research to examine the within-individual dynamics of emotional labour. Where this has been attempted, the study and theoretical construction of emotional labour has been approached from a gendered perspective.

Darkness as gendered accounts

Emotions and emotion work have traditionally been positioned as women's work. This is significant insofar as 'women's work' is commonly associated with gendered accounts of positive empathetic emotion, often accompanied by lower pay and status. And yet, such gendered accounts of emotional labour are casting a long shadow over more traditionally 'masculine' requirements to enact less servile emotional performances, and malestream academic concerns in business schools with the labour that men do.

Gendered job segregation has always been a feature of the workplace and is often cited as one of the most significant reasons why women's pay lags behind that of men. Such an attribution, however, calls for a consideration of what it is about so-called women's work that inappropriately enables employers to offer a reduced level of pay. For Guy and Newman (2004) the answer lies with the gendered perceptions of emotional labour. Starting with Hochschild's (1983) comparative analysis of the flight attendants and bill collectors, we are offered an emotionally gendered comparison (Erickson & Ritter, 2001) in a book dominated by the work of flight attendants and of empathetic performances. More important, the compassion that underlies empathetic performances is often assumed to come more easily to women than men – to arise as a natural component of their sex. Following this argument, the idea that women exhibit, handle and even 'feel' softer emotions quite naturally is taken to imply that emotional labour is not a 'skill', not real 'labour', and as such is outside the scope of proper renumeration (James, 1989; Leidner, 1993; Sutton, 1991). To this end emotional labour has tended to speak of 'the "softer" emotions, those required in relational tasks such as caring and nurturing, that disappear most often from job descriptions, performance evaluations and salary calculations' (Guy & Newman, 2004:289). Coupled with the servility implied by care, the effect has been to downgrade the occupational and financial claims of those such as nurses, HR specialists and front-line service staff whose emotional labour is seen as a central component of their occupational task (while effectively ignoring the fact that, in practice, emotional labour applies to both men's and women's work).

Nixon (2009) takes this argument a step further, claiming low-skilled men are actually deterred from 'low-skilled' work in today's job market because of the increasingly emotional nature of the job roles available in post industrial economies – where 'emotion' is used as a synonym for empathetic performances. In essence, the heavy, physical, dirty, manual, low-skilled work of the past has been subsumed by tertiary-sector work in which servility, cheer and smiles are key strategies for meeting ambitious sales targets in the face of 'demanding publics' (Williams, 2003) and abusive customers (Korczynski & Evans, 2013). In this sense, Nixon (2009) argues that low-skilled men are unwilling to 'lower themselves' to service with a smile, as it is an affront to their working-class masculinity (for examples see Mullen, 1993; Campbell, 2000; Connell, 2000; Roper, 1994). Emotional service work sits uneasily with masculine (mythical) cultures centred on 'physical prowess; toughness; homophobia; risk-taking; aggression and violent behaviour; a competitive spirit; a lack of emotional display [and] dispassionate instrumentalism' (McIvor, 2013:80–81).

In both Nixon (2009) and Guy and Newman's (2004) arguments, 'emotional labour' is seen as a highly influential factor in social and political terms, contributing to the gendered pay gap and high levels of unemployment amongst low-skilled men. And yet, both of these studies assume that 'emotional labour' is the performance of positive emotions in return for a wage. In other words, they are defining emotional labour as 'empathetic' or positive, thereby ignoring job roles and occupations that require antipathetic emotional labour often characterised by aggression and intimidation. Arguably, those roles that are characterised by the ability to perform negative emotions such as anger, fear and alarm, or, as Humphrey *et al.* (2008) refer to them, the work of 'social control agents' such as debt collectors, bailiffs, army sergeants, bouncers, all of which are more stereotypically associated with men's work or certainly as 'masculinity' at work. Collinson and Hearn (1996:107) argue that work involving aggressive sales and entrepreneurial cultures of insurance and financial consultation coupled with competitiveness and ambition are more likely to foster 'manliness' in a nonmanual setting and that arguably this is because these roles allow for the exhibition of less empathetic forms of emotion management. Therefore, constructing emotional labour as 'women's work' is misleading as it prioritises empathetic performances characterised by servility, care and compassion over antipathetic performances characterised by intimidation, fear and aggression. For us, the point is to explore the dark side of emotional labour in its feminine and masculine forms, seeking accounts of positive, negative, empathetic and antipathetic performances by workers in accordance with and in opposition to the social ascriptions of their sex.

The dark side of emotional labour

To sum up, sociological studies have tended to marginalise dissonance as a concern, in favour of more Marxist forms of alienation, whilst psychological work has conceptualised dissonance as a causal link between the performance of emotional labour and its associated negative consequences. The result is research on emotional labour that has tended to paint a dark, gloomy picture of what it means socially, psychologically, economically and politically to exchange personal and private feelings and emotions for a wage. And so, you might be ask yourself, why have Routledge commissioned a book entitled *The Dark Side of Emotional Labour*? What does this book have to offer that others have not already covered?

Well, here lies the interesting paradox. The arguably pessimistic, dark and negative theoretical constructs, conceptualisations and consequences born out of 30 years of emotional labour research across disciplines have been the product of empirical research contexts that are, in the main, characterised by positivity, smiles, cheer and agreeableness. The flight attendants Hochschild observed and interviewed spent their days working to suppress their own feelings of exhaustion, frustration and fear whilst simultaneously enacting emotions to create a cheerful, carefree pleasurable experience for their passengers in line with the regulations prescribed by the airline. Positive interpersonal interactions such as this can be understood to be a product of the expression of *integrative* emotions (Diefendorff *et al.*, 2006) or the performance of *positive* (Rafaeli & Sutton, 1987) or *empathetic* (Korczynski, 2003) emotional labour. Occupational roles characterised by empathetic emotional labour performances form the empirical foundation of emotional labour research (for example: flight attendants (Tyler & Taylor, 2001; Williams, 2003); nurses (James, 1989; Bolton, 2000, 2005); beauty therapists (Sharma & Black, 2001); paralegals (Lively, 2002); call-centre operators (Taylor, 1998; Shuler & Sypher, 2000); tour reps (Guerrier & Adib, 2003); adventure guides (Sharpe, 2005); nursing home carers (Lopez, 2006); cruise ship crew (Tracy, 2000); Disneyland employees (Van Maanen, 1991); and academics (Ogbonna & Harris, 2004)). The asymmetry of the occupational contexts within which emotional labour research has been carried out has undoubtedly coloured and even skewed the way in which the construct has been theoretically framed and understood.

In this way, 30 years of academic research from across the disciplines has shied away from addressing, exploring and dealing with occupational contexts and interactions that are defined and textured by difficult, uncomfortable, dirty and sometimes traumatising emotions and feelings (some notable exceptions include McMurray & Ward, 2014; Chiappetta-Swanson, 2005;

Sanders, 2004). Informed by our own research into the emotional labour undertaken by doctor's receptionists (aka the dragon behind the desk) (Ward & McMurray, 2011) and Samaritans (a voluntary organisation dedicated to reducing suicide and improving emotional well-being) (McMurray & Ward, 2014) we began to question the empirical basis of existing emotional labour research and to acknowledge the darker reality of a significant number of occupations that involve emotion management.

This is where this book makes its focus. *The Dark Side of Emotional Labour* moves away from the existing debates around dissonance, alienation, exploitation and gender (as a lens) to privilege the lived experience of emotional labourers engaged in the darker side of emotional labour performances. By this we mean those who undertake work that requires them to interact with, perform, manage and/or cope with emotions and feelings that are socially and psychologically difficult, dirty, inappropriate and sometimes traumatising. Taking this approach, we offer a variety of new empirical data gathered through targeted interviews with those in 'darker' occupations but also reinterpretations of existing studies, ethnographic accounts, TV documentaries and on-screen portrayals. We have also attempted to push beyond traditional conceptualisations of 'light' and 'dark', 'good' and 'bad' (Linstead et *al.*, 2014; McCabe, 2014; Muhr & Rehn, 2014) to offer some interesting occupational juxtapositions to illustrate a number of emotional labour constructs; examples include bouncers and primary school teachers as performers of negative or antipathetic emotional labour (Chapter 2); veterinary surgeons and home care workers sharing a predisposition for the darker side of caring in the form of emotional capital (Chapter 6); and an HR director and a flight attendant working to absorb organisational pain to prevent the spread of emotional toxicity (Chapter 5). Through these comparisons we seek to shed light on a number of questions. Specifically, what is the reality of engaging with darker emotions and feelings in different contexts? Why, and with what consequences, have they been overlooked or marginalised by existing literatures across disciplines?

In summary, *The Dark Side of Emotional Labour* attempts to provide academics, organisational practitioners and a wider interested audience with textured accounts of work that deals with dark, uncomfortable, dirty and sometimes toxic emotions. In so doing, we introduce a number of marginalised concepts that have been born out of Hochschild's original insights and subsequent research, including dirty work (McMurray & Ward, 2014; Hughes, 1962, 1984; Chiappetta-Swanson, 2005; Ashforth & Kreiner, 1999); emotional neutrality (Ward & McMurray, 2011; Smith & Kleinman, 1989); emotional capital (Cahill, 1999; Voronov & Vince, 2012) and toxic emotions (Frost, 2003). Moreover, we consider what is to be done with darker emotional work, in terms of both the management of such work and the care of workers who labour on the dark side of emotional labour.

Chapter overviews

This monograph is informed by almost two decades of qualitative research spanning hundreds of hours of observations and interviews with those in a variety of occupational roles from front-line service staff to managing directors, temporary workers to members of privileged professions, and across the divides of public, private and voluntary organising. In places these are supplemented by extracts from TV documentaries, fictional shows, films and other published ethnographies where it was felt that the inclusion of such examples would aid understanding or further contextual generalisation. Where, as in the majority of cases, our own data are employed, we have shown and discussed our written accounts with those who were interviewed or observed. We have done this (wherever possible) to ensure that our re-presentations still chime with the lived experiences and understanding of those involved. We thank all those (mostly anonymised) workers for the access, time and wisdom they shared with us. We note, however, that any mistakes, omissions or inaccuracies in what follows are entirely the responsibility of us, the authors. The remainder of the book is structured as follows.

Chapter 2: Paid to scare or care? The invisibility of antipathetic emotional labour

In this chapter we contend that negative emotional performances have been effectively written out of both emotional labour studies and the jobs market in favour of more positive, empathetic or even neutral forms (see Chapter 3). Accordingly, we examine whether or not there continues to be a role for negative emotional labour performances in organising contexts, particularly those performances intended to incite fear and intimidation. Drawing on the recent popular TV documentary *Can't Pay? We'll Take It Away!* and primary interview data with police officers, primary school teachers, prison officers and doormen and -women, we ask: why are we less willing to talk about the use and usefulness of negative emotions such as anger, intimidation and threat in the pursuit of organisational goals? And, what is life like for those whose work is purposefully characterised by fear, intimidation and control?

Chapter 3: Absent emotion? Remaining neutral in the face of abuse

In this chapter we consider what happens when workers are faced with situations in which the performance of neither empathy nor antipathy is appropriate. We have in mind those times where customers are abusive, staff are errant and bosses are unreasonable. We describe contexts in which workers are faced with irrational and unpleasant encounters but are still required to maintain professional performances that neither condemn nor condone the acts of others. Reviewing the experiences of hotel owners, HR managers, carers, veterinarians and prison officers, we explore the performance of what we call *emotional neutrality*. We consider how and why it is that workers choose to present neutral emotional performances that effectively hide the hurt, frustration, anger, pain, disdain, pity or indeed empathy they actually feel. We note that on the one hand emotionally neutral performances are a way of coping with the contradictions inherent in modern service economies where abuse is tolerated because the consumer is king, while on the other hand certain neutral performances act as a caring response to the pain and difficulties of others.

Chapter 4: Dealing in emotional dirty work

At one time or another most of us are required to undertake work that is deemed dirty. Traditionally tasks were deemed dirty if they involved interaction with physical contaminants, socially undesirable situations or contexts associated with sin. In this chapter we consider the conditions under which individuals might be said to undertake emotionally dirty work. Drawing on the experiences of those working in the public, private and voluntary sectors, we explain why people take on emotionally dirty work, how they make sense of it, and what they themselves get out of it. This reveals a complex picture of the dark side of emotional labour in which work that others see as undesirable, dangerous and tainted is described by workers with a sense of job satisfaction and pride. Finally, we show how individuals and occupations reframe and renarrate what it means to be involved in emotional dirty work such that it is seen as a positive social good.

Chapter 5: "Who will we go to with our problems?": emotional pain and the threat of toxicity

Organisational life can be painful because customers can be unreasonable, because some coworkers are manipulative, because bosses ask for the impossible, because our efforts can go unrewarded, because the experience of work can be disempowering and because dealing with the emotions of self and other can be exceedingly, even unremittingly, demanding. In this chapter we outline an argument that positions emotional pain as an inevitable by-product of organisational life. By drawing on our own interviews with cabin crew, an HR manager and a lawyer, as well as illustrative stories of emotional distress covered in the media, we support Frost (2003) in demonstrating that such organisational pain has the potential to turn into something more sinister and arguably more dangerous: emotional toxicity. We note also that the danger of toxicity is often averted by those unsung emotion workers that Frost (2003) identifies as 'toxin handlers'.

Chapter 6: "Some people can do it and some people can't": emotional capital as exposure, experience and praxis

Why do we each have different reactions, tolerances and capacities when it comes to performing emotional labour? Do different life experiences predispose different people to undertake work in particular emotional contexts, and, relatedly, do those experiences mean that some people are better equipped to cope with the light and dark that accompany emotional labour? This chapter begins to tackle these crucial questions by introducing, defining and exploring the concept of 'emotional capital'. Through analysis of spoken accounts of emotion at work from a veterinary surgeon and from care workers, we are able to identify three key factors in the development of emotional capital: exposure, experience and practice.

Chapter 7: Emotional labour and the ethics of care

In this final chapter we consider the responsibilities managers might have for the dark side of emotional labour. Specifically, we ask whether managers and employers have an ethical responsibility for the processes and effects of the emotional labour from which they profit. In so doing, we seek to open up the discussion of ethics and responsibility from the rather limited rationalised accounts of economic imperative and self-interest toward a discourse that recognises that organisations do and should care. We invite consideration of the multitude of ways in which different organisational actors are dependent on one another and whether such dependency necessitates care of others. Our position is that dependence does imply responsibilities and that care is a natural (if often forgotten) part of organising. From this standpoint we then go on to consider what an ethics of care might look like when applied to the dark side of emotional labour.

2 Paid to scare or care?

The invisibility of antipathetic emotional labour

'Come on don't be such a wimp. You've got to be more intense – where is that urgency in your voice?'

(Sutton, 1991:255)

We all manage our emotions on a daily basis. More often than not we do this to avoid conflict, discord and upset, as well as to protect, reassure and excite those around us. These microperformances of emotion management are the social glue (Raz, 2002) that helps maintain a light, cheerful easiness to our social relationships. This ability to manage our emotions and to sustain a particularly positive outward countenance that produces an emotional reaction in others is not, however, the preserve of our personal lives. As Hochschild (1983:7) famously illustrates, this ability to coordinate 'mind and feeling' has not escaped the attention of those who employ us. And yet, performing these positive emotions is just one way in which we manage the way that we feel and the way that others feel around us. Just as we have an ability to make others laugh, smile or feel happy, safe or excited, so too do we have the ability to make them feel scared, anxious, intimidated and distressed. We might shout at our children for misbehaving or adopt an authoritative tone when we complain in a restaurant. Controlling and managing our feelings in this way can put a temporary stop to the 'easiness' of social interactions to make things difficult, awkward and demanding.

This form of emotional labour, known as antipathetic emotional labour, is perhaps less talked about today than is its empathetic variant, but it is nonetheless a form of emotion management and one that Hochschild herself introduced in *The Managed Heart* through her presentation of the emotional labour of bill collectors. Although this form of emotional labour is introduced alongside the more well-known empathetic form (as epitomised in the work of the flight attendant), there is a distinct paucity of empirical research and literature that focuses on the usefulness of this type of emotion management. Indeed, the empirical marginalisation of contexts in which negative emotions have an exchange value has meant that the nature of such work, including the lived experiences and consequences for those paid to undertake it, remains invisible and unspoken from an academic perspective.

In this chapter we contend that negative emotional performances have been effectively written out of both emotional labour studies and the jobs market in favour of more positive or empathetic or even neutral forms (see Chapter 3). Accordingly, we examine whether there continues to be a role for negative emotional labour performances in organising contexts, particularly those performances intended to incite fear and intimidation. Drawing on the recent popular TV documentary *Can't Pay? We'll Take It Away!* and on primary interview data with police officers, primary school teachers, prison officers and doormen and -women, we ask: why are we less willing to talk about the use and usefulness of negative emotions such as anger, intimidation and threat in the pursuit of organisational goals? And, what is life like for those whose work is purposefully characterised by fear, intimidation and control? In concluding, we position antipathetic emotional labour as a strategic form of emotion management within a variety of occupational contexts. However, we also acknowledge the extent to which it has become an invisible and unspoken form of emotional labour – not only in practice but in theory. Consequently, we call for more empirical research into occupational contexts characterised by or involving negative emotional labour performances and for future research and theorising to shine a light on the use and usefulness of such emotions in the contemporary workplace, giving voice to those who are paid to work with and are subjected to dark, difficult and uncomfortable emotions and encounters that the rest of us actively avoid.

Antipathetic emotional labour

The concept of emotional labour has captured the imagination and sparked the interest of academics from a variety of disciplines, including psychology, sociology, nursing and communication studies, leading to a plethora of publications, studies and alternative definitions. The fundamental idea of employees routinely manipulating, managing and controlling both their own emotions and the emotions of those with whom they interact (customers, colleagues or patients) has enchanted these disciplines. Despite the variance in perspective and approach that each of these disciplines brings to bear on the study of emotional labour, they are connected by the tendency to focus on occupational contexts characterised by positive emotional displays (e.g. Van Maanen's [1991] study of Disneyland workers; Williams's [2003] and Taylor & Tyler's [2000] studies of flight attendants; Sharpe's [2005] work with adventure guides; and Sharma & Black's [2001] investigations of beauty therapists). These literatures have both implicitly and explicitly focused on occupations characterised by the expression of positive emotions as tools of influence because they are assumed to bring about organisational benefit, in the spirit of customer service, in the form of profit and reputation.

By contrast, negative emotional performances have received much less attention. Service interactions characterised by negative feelings such as anger and fear are said to involve 'differentiating emotions' (Dieffendorff *et al.*, 2006) through performances synonymously identified as antipathetic (Korczynski, 2003) or negative emotional labour (Rafaeli & Sutton, 1987). Humphrey *et al.* (2008) use the term 'social control agents' to describe archetypal antipathetic emotional labourers such as police officers, debt collectors and security guards, as they are 'required to express emotions that most people do not enjoy expressing, such as anger or irritation' (Humphrey, 2013:85). And yet, despite the emergence of a vocabulary to describe work with negative emotions, there has been very little empirical research on the emotional labour of those expected to display negative emotions as part of their job role. This is not to say that there have not been studies that touch upon or include accounts of employees making use of negative emotions within the workplace (examples include Tracy & Scott, 2006; Tracy, 2005), but none have made the management and expression of negative emotions their focus. With this in mind, it is important to spend a little time reviewing what little empirical research there has been in this area, specifically Sutton's (1991) work on debt collectors and Rafaeli and Sutton's (1991) comparative analysis of the emotional manipulation strategies of bill collectors and criminal interrogators.

The use of negative emotions at work

Training and working as a debt collector, Sutton found that the organisation worked hard to manipulate the inner feelings of the debt collectors so that they became congruent with their espoused values. This often meant that debt collectors were encouraged to perceive and treat debtors as bad people, as Sutton's account testifies (1991:260) in respect of the advice given by a trainer:

> 'Start giving her grief' and 'Get mean'. He told me after the call, 'Don't think of her as a nice person. Think of her as a bill you've got to collect.'

Debt collectors are tutored both in the necessary absence of empathy and in the need to focus on the goal or task at hand, namely the retrieval of funds. The debtor is objectified ("think of her as a bill"), and the preferred performance is one framed in terms of giving grief. Then there were what Rafaeli and Sutton (1991) described as 'emotional contrast strategies'. Observing the work of bill collectors and criminal interrogators, they noted what were effectively 'good cop-bad cop' performances through which agents created a perceptual contrast that accentuated either positivity or negativity. In other words, by playing different roles or parts at different stages of the interaction with clients, the emotional labourer was able to manipulate the latter in order to achieve the task or goal (e.g. reclaim funds or elicit desired information).

The paucity of literatures of this type makes it difficult to draw any emergent themes in relation to the way organisations make use of negative emotions, but perhaps there is something to be said of the performativity of power relations when contrasted with more empathetic performances. The discussions of Rafaeli and Sutton (1991), Sutton (1991) and Hochschild (1983) regarding negative emotional labour share an implicit narrative of power. Emotional labour is in itself a study of the way in which organisations attempt to control and commodify individual feelings for organisational benefit, which is contingent on the emotional labourer's control of both her own and her customer's feelings. For Rafaeli and Sutton (1991:750), negative or unpleasant emotions are often used as 'tools of social influence, especially when they have more power than those they are trying to influence'. Hochschild also alludes to this idea by comparing the power difference between flight attendants and passengers, to bill collectors and debtors.

> Whereas a flight attendant is encouraged to elevate the passenger's status by lowering her own, a bill collector is given permission to puff himself up, to take the upper hand and exercise a certain license in dealing with others. One collector who disavowed such posturing himself claimed that it was common in other agencies he had worked for. 'A lot of these collectors just yell at people like they're taking something out on them. A lot of them get to feel like they're big shots.'
>
> (Hochschild, 1983:144)

Such observations raise important questions about the nature of the relationships between emotional labourers and their customers and the emotional tone of the service encounter, not to mention the gender assumptions that underpin such role performances (see later discussion). Interactions characterised by empathy, cheer and pleasantness require the emotional labourer to assume a position of servility to create an 'enchanting myth of consumer sovereignty' (Korczynski & Ott, 2004), whereas encounters characterised by intimidation, fear and aggression require the emotional labourer to feel, present or enact a superior position of authority and control, thereby dispelling any illusion that the organisation is anything but powerful. There continues to be a gap in our understanding and appreciation of what it means to perform antipathetic emotional labour in return for a wage, whether there are any consequences of such performances and, if so, how they are experienced. We turn now to explore the extent to which negative emotions can play a useful role in organisational life.

Framing the use of negative emotions at work

Following Sutton's (1991) and Hochschild's (1983) approach in researching antipathetic emotional labour, we undertook an analysis of job descriptions for debt collectors. A search for job descriptions on recruitment websites for debt collectors—the archetypal occupation associated with the performance of this kind of emotional labour—makes it apparent that there is something of a discrepancy between the way the jobs are described by employers on the one hand and academic researchers on the other. Where Hochschild (1983:5) noted that a negative 'emotional style of offering' (Hochschild, 1983:5) is a characteristic of this type of work, there appears to be no allusion to this within any of the job descriptions our searches returned. Take, for example, this job description for a 'Field Agent' that we found on a well-known recruitment website:

> *Acme Debt Collection is a major UK reconnection company specialising in the financial and utility industry, supporting our clients in re-establishing contact with their customers. We are urgently recruiting field agents in the [location omitted] area, due to rapid expansion, to join our successful team of agents.*
>
> *This is a field based role and you will be required to visit customers, both residential and commercial, for the purposes of resolving unpaid bills and or to collate information regarding the customer through routine enquiries, you will be required to assist our clients in reengaging with their customers and may be required to collect payments offering various payment options and schemes on their behalf.*
>
> *You will also be required to attend court in order to obtain warrants and will work with 3rd parties (locksmiths and qualified gas and electrical engineers) to carry out a warrant visit where an engineer will remove a gas/electrical meter and install a pre-payment meter.*
>
> *Our Agents are target driven and work on a salary and performance related bonus/commission structure. All agents are required to travel as and when required which may solve the occasional overnight stay away from home.*
>
> *Applicants must be flexible with regards to the hours of work and must possess strong communication skills and the ability to show empathy and be assertive.*
>
> (Sampled from a recruitment website on November 26, 2013. Pseudonyms used to protect anonymity.)

All of the advertisements we considered were bereft of the negative and often complex emotions reportedly involved in collecting debt as described in the literature (Hochschild, 1983; Rafaeli & Sutton, 1987; Sutton, 1991) and as portrayed in popular TV series such as the BBC's *The Sheriffs are Coming* and Channel5's *Can't Pay? We'll Take It Away!*. Such sources recount the need for intimidation and threatening behaviours, along with an ability to remain calm and authoritative in the face of debtors' lies, sob stories, aggression, violence, emotional turmoil and distress. While task focus is emphasised in recruitment literature ('our agents are target driven') and the customer-facing nature of the role is explicit ('you will be required to visit customers'), the need to manage negative emotions and antipathetic emotional performances is absent. We get little of the poignancy and emotional depth that is apparent in fly-on-the-wall television programmes such as *Can't Pay? We'll Take It Away!* in which the nature and effects of the debt collector's work are writ large for debtor and worker alike:

> On a dark rainy night, a week before Christmas, two High Court Enforcement Bailiffs, often referred to as 'Sheriffs', are sent to evict a family from their home in East London. The family had been issued an eviction notice at the end of their tenancy agreement more than 6 months prior but still remain in the property illegally. When they arrive the family resist the eviction by bolting the front door. There are two young children inside the property. After some hours of attempted negotiation one of the Sheriffs decides to take action.
>
> Standing with his face pressed against the front door he shouts to the tenant in a stern and threatening tone:
>
> *'If you don't open the door we're going to break the glass. . . . I'm giving you two minutes and then we break the glass.'*
>
> The Sheriff's threats are ignored and so he takes a crow bar from the van and forcibly enters the property. The family are given two hours to leave their home before they head off into the night and the Sheriffs change the locks to prevent them from re-entering.
>
> In a follow up interview the Sheriff explains how he feels about the situation:
>
> 'We've put an immigrant family out on the street two to three days before Christmas. They hadn't even got their Christmas tree up. They'll have no presents and nowhere to go. It's pissing it down with rain and they'll be really unhappy. How can that be a good result?'
>
> (*Can't Pay? We'll Take It Away!*, Channel 5, Series One, Episode Two, originally aired March 3, 2014)

Emotion and negative emotional performances are central to this account. The ability to employ a stern voice and to threaten physical action ('we're going to break the glass') speak to an ability to 'induce or suppress feeling in order to sustain the outward countenance that produces the proper state of mind in others' (Hochschild, 1983:7). This is the very epitome of emotional labour.

Given the place of antipathetic emotional labour in such work, why is it not mentioned in job descriptions? It can hardly be because such emotions are not deemed useful. In the case just described, physical force and antipathetic labour succeeded where court orders and negotiation alone had failed. Resorting to force and intimidation had demonstrable use value insofar as the will of the property owner and the legal system were successfully imposed. As Hochschild has noted, debt collectors are tutored in the need to create feelings of urgency, intimidation and alarm precisely because such emotions evoke a sense of fear in the debtor, encouraging him to 'pay up' or leave, thereby benefiting the organisation:

> The rule in this agency was to be aggressive. One novice said 'My boss comes into my office and says, "Can't you get madder than that?"' "Create alarm!" – that's what my boss says. Like an army sergeant, the boss sometimes said his employees were not men unless they mustered up a proper degree of open outrage.
>
> (Hochschild, 1983:146)

In this sense, the emotional abilities and resilience of debt collectors and sheriffs are successfully employed as part of the harsh masculinised (see later discussion) organisational realities of debt collection. And yet there is reluctance for organisations to admit to or speak of the usefulness of less empathetic forms of emotional labour; they appear to be an unpalatable organisational reality. Indeed, some job descriptions we encountered suggested that empathy should be used to mask the harsher realities of antipathetic labour, such that candidates 'must possess strong communication and negotiation skills with the ability to show empathy whilst being assertive' (Acme Debt Collection). This is work on the dark side of emotional labour, not because it is negative or without use but because it is intended to go unseen – hidden from public and corporate view.

When we talk of emotions at work, there is, then, a preference to speak to more positive or empathetic emotional encounters. At one level this preoccupation with empathetic emotional labour is perplexing given that Hochschild's (1983) *The Managed Heart* is actually a comparative analysis of the way both positive and negative emotions were utilised by Delta Airlines (and their associated agencies) in the 1970s. The airline was employing (mostly female) flight attendants to smile, laugh and attend to passengers' every need on board their aircraft whilst they simultaneously commissioned (mostly male) bill collectors to create alarm, urgency and fear to facilitate the payment of outstanding debts. This gendered divide in employment and practice speaks in part of the different tasks and context of each encounter – one predicated on what are assumed to be one-off short-term encounters with a specific goal (e.g. collection of final debt) and the other in which relations last for hours, are directed at repeat business and have a safety component (e.g. passenger welfare). What they share is an exchange value. Like it or not, negative emotions can and do have a positive role to play in organisational contexts. As considered later, they are used to enforce the law, achieve organisational goals, turn a profit and control situations. This 'use' is frequently overlooked in the extant literature on emotional labour, given the preference for studying empathetic performances. In addition, little is made of the physical threats to life or of the intimidation and the abuse that are a likely reality of this type of work. The remainder of this chapter focuses on our interviews with bouncers, a police officer and a prison officer who share the lived reality of performing and embodying antipathetic emotional labour on a day-to-day basis. Our analysis of their accounts of such work highlights four key themes: that this type of antipathetic emotional labour is often performed against a backdrop of personal fear; that it often takes place in extreme contexts; that the ability to 'scare' others is complex and achieved through direct and indirect intimidation strategies; and that being paid to 'scare' in these contexts often comes at a high personal cost.

Fear and control of self

The performance of emotional labour is as much about managing your own emotions as it is about managing the feelings, behaviours and actions of others. In the case of antipathetic emotional labour, particularly in extreme circumstances, this often means that workers suppress their own fear and anxiety in order to control others. Allan, an experienced bouncer who now runs his own security firm, poetically illustrates this battle for control in a dramatic life or death situation:

> I have been threatened with knives and stabbed a couple of times but being threatened with a gun was a different feeling to the knife. Everything dropped out of me. You know if he fires that gun it doesn't matter how far away you are. I knew I had to stand there and not show any signs of weakness. It was a weird sensation . . . you know some nights when you go outside and you can hear trees rustling and cars going by and then other nights there is nothing – just quiet – it was like that.
>
> (Allan, bouncer)

In this situation Allan had to fight hard against his instincts to turn and run. Instead, he chose to *'stand there and not show any signs of weakness'*. In Hochschild's terms, he suppressed his own fear and desire to turn and flee and instead induced a sense of calm in himself that led the gunman to believe he had the upper hand in this situation, which prevented the situation from escalating to the point where people were hurt. Allan explained to us that he allowed the gunman to walk away into the crowded nightclub before informing the police and later going back in with a team of other bouncers to tackle the gunman to the ground and make the situation safe. Where sheriffs put their negative emotional labour to use in the retrieval of property, Allan employs it in the protection of self and others.

Tommy, a bouncer with more than 20 years' experience working 'the doors', explains how his relationship with fear has changed over time as a consequence of his exposure to situations in which he felt scared. His ability to avoid being overwhelmed and overcome by his own fear is a key part of his ability to perform antipathetic emotional labour in these extreme contexts:

> the number of times that I've gone into situations where I've thought whoa there's going to be some trouble here, I'm in trouble here and I've been threatened . . . this is in the early days . . . when I've just held my ground and I've been scared, you'd be a fool if you weren't scared because nobody wants to get pasted [beaten up], but knowing that you can't run away, nobody else is going to do it, you've got to be there and you've got to do it and you just . . . I would describe it as getting used to being scared you know . . . it's not that you lose your fear, you just get used to being scared . . . the same as I suppose a runner gets used to being tired and . . . you get fitter and in a way you get psychologically fitter by being used to being scared and in the end you get adrenaline . . . I wouldn't describe it as fear.
>
> (Tommy, bouncer)

Through exposure (see Chapter 6), Tommy has managed to turn his own fear into something more positive and useful to the point that he now experiences as adrenaline inducing situations that would once have terrified him. No longer are feelings of fear something to be anxious or worried about; instead, they are something to be celebrated, an attestation of emotional fitness in the context of door work. Similarly, Allan's account of his internal dialogue whilst being verbally abused attests to the ways in which experiences that many of us would find difficult become humorous and even enjoyable for those who are paid to undertake such work:

> I enjoy the job . . . it's not the best paid job in the world . . . you're lucky to get minimum wage . . . and you're putting yourself on the front line . . . people want to abuse you . . . assault you . . . like one bloke said to me 'Your Mum's a whore. I shagged your Mum last weekend.' I find that entertaining because in my head I'm thinking 'I really hope you didn't mate, my Mum died when I was five.' . . . you've got to be pretty thick skinned on the door . . . they call you disgusting names, they try to egg you on as far as they can to push and push and push and see whether you'll snap.
>
> (Allan, bouncer)

Working with the negative emotions of others can be both challenging ('they call you disgusting names') and rewarding ('I enjoy the job'). Note that there is a distinction to be made between working with the negative emotions of others and offering negative or antipathetic emotional performances as a worker. In the cases described, negative emotions provide the context within which work takes place. Both Allan and Tommy are on the receiving end of others' emotional provocations, in response to which they perform something approximating emotional neutrality (see Chapter 3). They work to control themselves in the face of another's aggression, antipathy and attempts to 'egg you on . . . and see whether you'll snap' (this is to be contrasted with the work of the sheriffs who sought to evoke discomfort and compliance through their own presentation of antipathetic labour in evicting debtors). In such contexts workers are opened up to verbal and physical threat. Two examples will suffice. The first is from a reality TV show in which two bailiffs are sent to repossess a man's car and are met with a barrage of abuse and threats (opening with the threats of the debtor):

> *'Don't fucking talk to me like I'm some sort of dickhead 'cos I'll take your head off . . . I'll kill you!'*
> At this point he takes a crowbar from the back of the car and smashes the windscreen of the repossessed vehicle, before continuing with:
> *'You come to my house and treat me like a gang of shit. I'll fucking take a piece of you. I'll fucking rip every one of you to bits. . . . '*
> In a follow up interview one of the bailiff's commented:
> *'Quite often threats are made in that manner. We've had quite a few threatening to throw bricks out the window at us . . . and you find yourself just laughing it off really . . . but it can turn out that they will do what they're threatening to do.'*
> (*Can't Pay? We'll Take It Away!*, Channel 5, Episode One,
> Series One, originally aired on February 24, 2014)

Our second account offers an example where threats become real and there is no possibility of 'laughing it off'. For Jackie, a bouncer, the negative intent of another results in a physical attack:

> I actually got stabbed, but at the time I didn't realise because . . . I was wearing a stab vest and it was a good job I was because I felt three blows to my back and never thought nothing of it and then . . . somebody said . . . you've got rips in your jacket. I took my jacket off and there were blade marks in my coat where it had gone straight through my coat. . . . I hit the floor like a tonne of bricks and just burst out crying because all I could think about were my two boys that were still at home . . . that really was a scary night. Scary as hell!
> (Jackie, bouncer)

Here threats are made real ('I actually got stabbed'), and there is no sense of labour or performance after the fact as Jackie 'just burst out crying'. Fear arises not so much in the event but on reflection, as her own physical fragility and the well-being of her two boys intrude upon her thoughts and work. Although bailiffs and door and security staff might learn to enjoy parts of their work – even parts that many others would shy away from – they are undoubtedly engaging in work which is challenging emotionally and sometimes dangerous physically. It requires emotional performances and control because it can be 'as scary as hell' and because workers can be injured or killed in the conduct of such work (on July 3, 2013, a bailiff and an income officer were shot in Brixton, London, whilst attempting to evict a tenant). These contexts describe emotional resilience and control in the face of provocation. There are, however, times when those such as bouncers and police officers are called on to employ physical force as part of their labour.

Control of force

Hobbs *et al.* (2002) and others have spent much time documenting the contrasting nature of the daytime and nighttime economies with respect to regulation and policing. Indeed, it has been argued that 'as the day gives way to the night, the state relinquishes and devolves many of its policing duties to the bouncer' (Hobbs *et al.*, 2002:355), thereby handing over responsibility and discretion to enforce commercially defined 'discipline' to bouncers (Loader, 2000). For some it would appear that this responsibility equates to a need to 'downplay' their own use of physical force as part of their labour. Jackie, a female bouncer with more than ten years' experience providing security details and door work at a range of events, explains that, while using physical violence is not a tactic with which she is comfortable, it is one she is prepared to use within limits:

> don't get me wrong if somebody takes a swing for me, then I'm going to make sure I get a swing back. . . . I don't like doing that, I feel guilty if I have to hit somebody . . . I've actually been punched to the point where I've been knocked over and the only way I could get back up was to hit back out at them . . . because they went to kick me while I was lying on the floor and the only way I could get out of it was to swing my legs round and knock their legs from underneath them, so I knocked them over . . . rather than kicking them I knocked them over then that gave me the chance to get up.
>
> (Jackie, bouncer)

Jackie's 'guilt' as a consequence of using physical violence is testament to the extent to which her work is characterised by emotional labour performances. She has to suppress her feelings of guilt in order to carry out certain parts of her work that are intended to scare, enforce boundaries and retain control. She works to justify her use of force as a defence of self ('because they wanted to kick me') and downplay the aggression of her own acts ('I knocked them over . . . rather than kicking them') in much the same way job descriptions downplay the need for antipathetic labour. Yet to control one's emotions when under physical threat is, as described by Peter, a police officer, no easy matter:

> There was a burglary, two people were arrested. Then their mate starts walking up. . . . I sort of cordoned him off to one area and said 'Right, you can't go near there because we need to speak to you . . . blah blah blah.' He then starts to push me, so I sort of grabbed him and pushed him against a hedge and leaned on him. He then starts moving around, so I put my arms around him and he kicked out, putting my knee out to the left. It really hurt. Really hurt! And instant red mist!
>
> I thought right, well, I need to stop him doing that again, so I literally grabbed this guy and pushed him into the hedge and held him in the hedge. Stopped him doing anything else . . . it was red mist. And you know what? I could have got the baton out and batoned him . . . or a spray . . . all these things, whether you can or you can't, whether you're supposed to or not, you've got all these things on you . . . because the red mist clouds it all. I was quite well restrained and only pushed him in the hedge.
>
> (Peter, police officer)

We can hear from Peter's account that feelings of anger, pain and frustration ('the red mist') were clearly prevalent on this particular day at work. For Peter this highly individualised experience demonstrates the emotional intensity of life as a police officer. Perhaps more interesting, however, is the self-congratulatory summation of Peter's story – there is a sense of relief in his tone as he reminds himself that he had shown restraint at not letting the 'red mist' take control, of not having given into his primeval reaction to lash out with physical violence. In the heat of the moment, Peter's feelings of anger rose dangerously close to the surface, but he managed to control and contain them in a way that allowed him to continue complying with the behavioural norms expected of the police force.

Prison Officer Graeme's account of a frightening and dangerous attack at work also illustrates the importance of emotional control with respect to personal safety:

> one day these two lads were sitting in their cell having a bit of a chit chat. I was on the landing. The fella who was running the workshop phoned us up and said can you get Johnny (prisoner) to come down here. So I went 'yes no problem' and went to see Johnny. 'Johnny, you are wanted down on the workshops.' 'I am not going.' So I said 'Johnny, I am giving you a direct order. Go to the workshop, get down there.' And this con just flew off the bed, grabbed us round the throat and pushed us against the wall and said 'I am not going.' OK fair enough, what can I do? I have got 136 prisoners here. I am not going to ring

the alarm bell now it's all over with. . . . I just went up to the office and phoned the boss downstairs and said, 'Look this is what has just happened. I am not ringing the bell now. It's all over with. When everybody comes back from the workshops, they have had their dinner and gone to bed, we are going to open him up again and he is going to isolation because I am not having it . . . he probably sat there all morning thinking 'I got away with that.'

(Graeme, prison officer)

In further discussions relating to how Graeme experienced this incident, he told how he felt:

Pretty isolated and probably scared because anything could have happened there. I could have been dragged in the cell; I could have been a hostage, anything. So that's probably one of the reasons why it was best left until there are plenty of staff about. Let's get everybody locked up and then let's go and take him out of here.

(Graeme, prison officer)

Rather than 'ringing the bell' to call for backup and support, Graeme chose to stifle his fear and control his desire to act based on an assessment of what was best for both personal and institutional security. His analysis of the situation, despite his being scared, required him to be patient and to control his desire for redress ('he is going to isolation because I am not having it') in fear that a more immediate reaction might have led to further, more serious threats and acts of violence.

These accounts tell of work contexts that are alien to many of us. In a society dominated by tertiary-sector service workers, few of us have to deal with the brutal reality of social control work. For the most part these accounts speak to a need to control oneself in the face of fear, intimidation and physical aggression. Emotional labour presents as either the presentation of a neutral face (see Chapter 3) or the enactment of strength or intimidation. On occasions these emotional states are backed up by physical performances designed to assert or regain control. Where other emotional labourers are paid to uphold the myth of consumer sovereignty, those in enforcement roles are charged with effectively compelling people to do something they would not otherwise want do: to pay a debt, to leave a premises, to stand for an alleged crime. In such contexts antipathetic labour has a very definite exchange value. Even so, there appears to be tendency to play such accounts down, to justify the use of aggression as a necessary response to the negative emotions or actions of others. It is offered as a rational response to the negative emotional contexts in which the workers find themselves. And yet, there are occasions on which antipathetic labour is wielded proactively rather than in response to others' actions.

Intimidation

Eliciting information and accounts of proactive antipathetic emotional labour in the form of, say, intimidation is harder than you might expect. As already noted, there seems to be a reluctance on the part of those who engage in such work to admit this is what they do or to recount how they do it. Through careful analysis of our participants' accounts, we note that intimidation appears to be induced either overtly or ambiguously. Overt intimidation is behaviour undeniably designed to threaten, scare and repel. Emotive intimidation, on the other hand, is seemingly more ambiguous and works on socially constructed appreciations of complex social fears that seem to arise from threats to individual identity.

Overt Intimidation

For us, overt intimidation refers to strategies that are adopted to directly intimidate an individual on the basis of emotional-physical threats. They are intentional, scripted and rehearsed with a reasonable approximation of their effectiveness. Often such intimidation is enacted with the aid of specific props and repertoires. We offer three examples, starting with Allan's use of his highly trained dog:

> anywhere I go now I take a dog and they're all trained . . . if I tell them to bark they'll bark, if I tell them to foam at the mouth, they'll do it and then stop just on my command . . . and it's a lot more intimidating for a criminal or thug . . . to have a dog at the side of you.
>
> (Allan, bouncer)

Allan appreciates the impact his trained dogs will have on any intruder he might come across late at night. The dog serves as prop in the invocation of fear, uncertainty and threat in those whom Allan meets. The performance belongs to Allan insofar as it is he who commands the dog and uses it as an extension of his own will. The training and use of the dog is designed and scripted to be 'a lot more intimidating for a criminal or thug'. For Jackie, a five-foot-three-inch female bouncer, her uniform and physical stance are significant in her presentation of self in the context of being intimidating:

> don't get me wrong we can all be intimidating, I mean I have actually had people come up to me and say . . . 'you're so intimidating in your uniform' . . . I suppose I can do because we are supposed to stand in one particular . . . I don't know typical doorman stance . . . with the feet apart, hands in front of us, looking relaxed.
>
> (Jackie, bouncer)

Although Jackie is diminutive, her uniform is seen as 'intimidating'. But it is not just the uniform. Her presence is also a product of the 'doorman stance', designed to convey a sense of relaxed authority and preparedness. Jackie's costume and presentation front of house evokes an emotional response before she needs to speak. She embodies an antipathetic performance. To this end, Hobbs *et al.* (2002) talk of bouncers' use of bodily capital to communicate and support their ability and willingness to use physical force. Their observations focused on the ways in which door staff appeared to cultivate an 'authoritatively intimidating appearance and demeanour' (Hobbs *et al.*, 2002:357), mainly in the form of battle scars or a well-maintained and powerful physique.

There is, then, a sense in which occupational members orchestrate presentations of antipathetic labour. For bouncers it takes the form of a generalised dress code and a demeanour that pervades their work. For other occupations the orchestration of intimidation has quite specific triggers and contexts. Take for example Prison Officer Graeme's account of the 'Rapid Removal Team'. These staff are called upon to go into prisons or cells when order has broken down. This is an act of last resort:

> Rapid Removal Teams are trained for cell removals. I used to be on the team and you would call them in from home and say 'we have got a situation here we need some staff. Can you come in?' It [this situation] has gone past the point of having a chat. The situation needs to be resolved; they [errant prisoners] need to be taken out of there. So you get all kitted up in the protective gear, shields. . . . They [Rapid Removal Team] are all kitted out in shields and everything . . . helmets . . . we would march in an organised group so they [errant prisoners] can see what is coming, what the consequences are going to be. It is designed to make them think, 'I don't want any of this when that door opens.'
>
> (Graeme, prison officer)

What Graeme describes is the military-style orchestration of the Rapid Removal Team brought in to tackle out-of-control prisoners. Being kitted up in 'protective gear, shields . . . helmets' is required in part because, as Graeme went on to note, once you open the prison cell door out-of-control prisoners 'are going to be attacking you with table legs or whatever else they have managed to get their hands on'. In this sense, equipment is a matter of worker protection. But it is also props for intimidation designed to make prisoners think, 'I don't want any of this'. The guards march in a show of strength as a deliberate reflection of the fact that things have now 'gone past the point of having a chat' as prison officers use sanctioned restraint techniques to gain compliance and regain control. In all three cases, then, there is a sense of theatre insofar as props and repertoires are embodied by actors intent on eliciting a specific emotional response in others, as part of organisational concerns with control. That is not to say that intimidation was the mainstay of the workers' performances. Graeme, for example, was at pains to point out that such performances were the exception rather than norm. His training emphasised de-escalation wherever possible. And yet, as reluctant as he was to talk about it, it was also clear that there were times when explicitly antipathetic emotional performances had a useful role to play in organising. Our discussions of intimidation also revealed the usefulness of less overt strategies of intimidation.

Intimidation through uncertainty and absence

The above accounts speak of the ways in which props, repertoires and embodied physicality are used to intimidate others. Yet, through discussions with those whose work involves scaring others, we found that intimidation was also about uncertainty and absence. As considered in this section, workers would employ impression management strategies (Goffman, 1959), centred on silence and inaction, that were designed to create an uncertain sense of processes and outcomes in the mind of the audience. Such performances are of interest because silence and inaction, in contexts where one would expect much action in the form of physical and verbal confrontation, can be read as an emotional absence that elicits an uncertainty intended to be experienced as fear. Jackie is particularly aware of how important uncertainty is in her repertoire of intimidation:

> I'm five foot three . . . it makes people laugh because . . . they assume that whoever the bouncers are that night, they're going to be big guys or big girls and when they see me . . . it's not something they're expecting . . . *to me it's keeping them guessing* because with me being small *they don't know how I'm going to react if they start an argument or a fight* . . . and the last thing a guy wants . . . especially if he is six foot three . . . he doesn't want me putting him on his backside.
>
> (Jackie, bouncer)

Jackie is very much aware of the uncertainty her size and gender generate, particularly with male customers. She uses the fact that her physical identity does not conform to the expectations of a 'doorman' as a form of intimidation. By remaining silent and not reacting, she purposefully leaves space for reflection and uncertainty, which she feels is disconcerting for those who might consider challenging her and yet who fear the reputational and identity consequence of 'me putting him on his backside'.

Surprisingly, a very similar story emerged from one of our interviews with a primary school teacher. Clarissa explained how the policy in her school was for teachers not to shout or get angry at children regardless of their behaviour. She explained how, rather than shouting, she communicates her disapproval via a calm tone and a slow pace of voice, coupled with a long period of eye contact and authoritative body language and facial expressions. It is the silence and uncertainty that are allowed to grow in the absence of talk that becomes intimidating. Clarissa draws an interesting comparison between what she perceives to be genuine feelings of anger and that which is performed as antipathetic emotional labour:

> There is a difference between being genuinely mad which I think my class has probably seen four or five times . . . compared to me pretending that I'm mad which has got a much calmer, slightly [laughs], more intimidating effect. Because I look like I'm in so much control because my voice hasn't got any higher, I am just telling them the consequences and what will happen now. This has more effect.
>
> (Clarissa, primary school teacher)

Through the emotional labour lens, then, it is perhaps nonconformity to the display rules (Ekman, 1973) that is expected in a situation that is a source of uncertainty. If someone is not complying with the display and feeling rules, what else might she be capable of? We can read this into Allan's account of confronting a shoplifter who, although thwarted by the expected presence of a security guard, is discombobulated by Allan's unexpected intervention:

> We were just doing our shopping and I saw this guy running out of the main doors with the security guy chasing him, he was giving him the run around . . . going in one door and out the other . . . and I just couldn't help myself . . . I just stood in front of him. This is where the intimidation comes in . . . I said 'You go back in or I'll drag you in' . . . *I just stood there.*
>
> (Allan, bouncer)

Allan's behaviour is unexpected, unpredictable and intimidating. Unlike the security guard, he does not chase the thief but stands still, proffering an order based on uncertain authority and supported by the threat of physical intervention ('I'll drag you back in'). His subsequent silence invites the shoplifter to make a decision in the absence of certain knowledge as to what comes next – it has an emotional effect. We can see something similar in Ian's approach to handling a costly oversight in a car repair workshop:

> John had worked for us for a couple of months and had asked me for more responsibility. So, that week he had been asked to do the daily tyre order. Monday morning I arrived at the workshop but there was no sign of the tyre delivery. I called him into my office to give them a call to chase the order. His face turned a whiter shade of pale as he took the phone from my hand. I stared at him, knowing full well from his

reaction that this was not a mix up with the delivery but that he had forgotten to place the order. He stood in front of me, his face getting redder and redder. 'That is £2000 of work you have lost us,' I said calmly as I held eye-contact with him for what seemed like an age. I couldn't see the point in shouting at John, despite wanting to punch him. What was the point? He had got the message. All day he worked on his own, didn't even sit with the lads at tea break. He knew I was furious, so he kept his distance. This is just the way I manage. I am not one for shouting the odds – less is more for making a point like this. He won't do it again.

(Ian, service manager)

Here Ian's management approach is to effectively withdraw his support from John in order to make him feel ostracised by the rest of the group. By calmly stating the consequences of John's oversight and maintaining his gaze for an uncomfortable length of time, Ian communicates his disappointment and anger without having to raise his voice or instigate formal disciplinary procedures. For Ian 'less is more' in the sense that it left John with space to reflect on his action but also a little perturbed at the potential burgeoning punishment that might be coming his way.

Harlow *et al.*'s (1995) account of intimidation evoked by the silence of a single manager on four women working together in a small office might be considered a darker extension of Ian's approach to punishing John:

> They [the four women] talked of the weekend and of the day's coming work. The man arrived, barely responded to greetings, and sat at his desk in silence. The women were gradually reduced to silence. He did not say a word, but the din of his presence, maleness and intimidation created a silence which was uneasy. The women felt they had been bullied.
>
> (Harlow *et al.* (1995:103)

Here silence is associated with intimidation and the emotional pain of bullying. The uncertainty that the silence produces, the unexpected disregard of polite norms of acknowledgement and conversation, threatens to create a toxic environment (see Chapter 5). It is disruptive such that others are manipulated into breaking off from their normal everyday behaviours. This apparently deliberative act of otherness unsettles the office but in a way that is difficult to articulate or complain about.

In each of these accounts, emotions were managed in a way that led to the absence of expected behaviours. This absence was purposeful in that it was performed as a strategy of intimidation in order to generate uncertainty. Such uncertainty makes space for reflection and consideration of possible outcomes, all of which lead to a potential threat to the identity, reputational capital and even safety of those to whom it is directed.

Conclusion

To conclude, negative emotions in organisational settings have been largely presented through the hostility triad (Pelzer, 2005): anger, disgust and contempt. In much of the prescriptive literature these have been states organisations should work to avoid or 'come through' as they have the potential to become toxic, contagious and inevitably disastrous (see Chapter 5). And yet, this apocalyptic view of negative emotions serves to overshadow the occasions, roles and contexts in which negative emotions become useful and are not therefore something that individuals and organisations catch or become victims of but are enacted for organisational ends. Society's preoccupation with an ideology of customer care and the related stigmatisation of negative emotions has rendered antipathetic emotional labour invisible in both the jobs market and academic research. Consequently, we call for further research into occupational and work contexts that require people to induce or suppress negative emotions in return for a wage, and to explore the consequences, strategies and outcomes of such work. Most important, we call for research that acknowledges the texture and complexity of this work, while also giving those who undertake it a voice to express the lived experiences of labouring on the dark side. With this in mind this chapter set out to explore two main questions: is there a role for antipathetic emotional labour in contemporary organisational contexts? What is life like for those whose work is characterised by fear, intimidation and control?

In the presentation of our interview data with prison officers, police, primary school teachers, service managers and bouncers, we analysed accounts that highlight the complexity, use and usefulness of antipathetic emotional labour in organisational contexts. In particular, debt collection and door security work involve a strategic use of antipathetic emotional labour, insofar as such labour facilitates the attainment of organisational goals. We also considered the manner in which these organisationally useful performances of negative emotion are then downplayed and reframed organisationally through, for example, the omission of references to antipathetic labour in job descriptions. Our point is that although organisations clearly benefit from the abilities of a workforce to perform antipathetic emotional labour, such labour seems to be written out of official accounts as an unpalatable organisational reality. It is denied, unspoken and hidden from both corporate and public view in favour of more empathetic or neutral depictions of the work. It is the extent to which this emotional, difficult, demanding and often unpleasant work is hidden from both public and corporate view that renders it work on the dark side.

In relation to our second question – the lived reality of performing antipathetic emotional labour – we presented two main themes. First, we considered the backdrop of fear and anxiety against which this type of emotional labour is often performed, including very real threats to life and personal safety. Here we argued that antipathetic emotional labourers are often called upon to suppress their own fears in order to induce fear and intimidation in others. Second, we explored the two ways in which intimidation can be induced in others: overtly and as a product of uncertainty. Intimidation through uncertainty and absence is also illustrative of the ways in which an absence of emotion can also be useful in organisational contexts – a point which we now seek to explore more fully in Chapter 3.

3 Absent emotion?

Remaining neutral in the face of abuse

'You leave your own emotions in the boot of your car or on the dashboard (when you arrive for a work shift).'

(Jennifer, Samaritan)

Should emotions be part of managing and organising? Are organisations to be viewed primarily as places of rationality, or is there space for feelings, too? Is it possible to rationalise and remove emotions even when those external to the organisation (i.e. customers) are unreasonable or abusive? A search of Google suggests that such questions remain pertinent to the business of organising in the twenty-first century. Type in the phrase 'leave your emotions at the door' and you will be rewarded with more than 130 million hits (January 2015) covering academic papers, opinion pieces, blogs, testimonies, sales pitches, self-help guides and images. Many of the blogs and advice columns that appear in the first few pages assert that the evocation to 'leave your emotions at the door' is unreasonable, even impossible. Emotions, they argue, are an unavoidable part of who we are. An article in *Forbes* enquires:

> Have you cried in the work restroom or at a meeting with your boss? How about awkwardly trying to comfort a coworker in tears? Or maybe you've been the culprit or victim of explosive, finger-wagging, temples-pulsing anger? If you're nodding 'yes,' it's not so surprising. Despite the corporate expectation to check your emotions at the door, tempers and tear ducts continue to swell in workplaces everywhere. We're all human, after all.
>
> (Goudreau, 2013)

Such accounts imply that emotions are an inevitable facet of the human condition. This being the case, the 'corporate expectation to check your emotion at the door' (Goudreau, 2013) seems impossible, even illogical. Why then does the idea of dividing rationality and emotion persist?

In answering this question, we take a brief look back at the work of Max Weber and the ideal of an efficient bureaucracy unfettered by the apparent distractions of emotion. We consider the place of rationality in organisations, both as a managerial myth and as a mechanism of emotional control. From here it is quickly apparent that, far from being removed from organising, emotions are an essential part of the services we sell. Indeed, as customers demand our smiles, forbearance, empathy and good humour, so the organisations of which we are part have sought to manage and control the emotions we perform. Generally such performances take the form of emphatic labour and, more unusually, antipathetic labour (as discussed in Chapter 2). There are, however, occasions on which neither of these performances is appropriate, where the worker must instead perform *emotional neutrality* (Smith & Kleinman, 1989; Ward & McMurray, 2011).

As considered later, the performance of emotional neutrality, as a form of emotional labour, is intended to convey an absence of feeling on the part of the worker. By its very nature – the presentation of absence – emotional neutrality is difficult to observe. At first glance such performances appear to adhere to the Weberian rational ideal of organising without feelings, as workers offer no hint of emotion in the face of unwelcome interactions or abuse. In this chapter we consider why workers offer these performances of emotional neutrality, particular as part of service encounters. Drawing on Korczynski's (2001) conceptualisation of the 'customer-orientated bureaucracy', we consider how the rationalising myths of consumer sovereignty clash with the ideals of bureaucratic efficiency to leave service workers in a dark and unenviable position between competing rationalities that prevent the labourer from displaying the hurt, frustration, anger, pain, disdain, pity or indeed empathy that they really feel. It is our contention that under such circumstances emotions are not in fact absent but instead hidden, as workers labour to conceal what they really feel. We explore why workers conceal such feelings through performances of neutrality and how they subsequently make sense of such dark encounters. We begin by considering the ways in which classical management theory sought to write emotion out of organising by presenting a rational, neutral and masculine face. This is followed by a partial acceptance of the need for certain limited emotional performances to meet the demands of consumers for effective service. We then consider how the contradictions inherent in the demands of our bureaucracies and the demands of consumers open up workers to abuse and how such abuse serves as a major context for the performance of neutrality. We begin by reminding ourselves how modern organisations can still be considered bureaucracies and what bureaucracy implies in terms of the march of rationality.

Rationality and the absence of emotion

Every organisation is a bureaucracy insofar as it is composed of rules, hierarchy and limits to legitimate authority. Bureaucracy is 'the means of transforming social action into rationally organized action' (Barker, 1993:410 citing Weber, 1978:987). Weber's (1946) account of the modern bureaucratic organisation is one in which individuals operate in strict accordance with objective rules, within the confines of the authority invested in their position and without fear or favour when interacting with clients. Individuals are appointed to their roles according to the merits of their abilities. Members are arranged hierarchically, with those at the bottom of the organisation having very limited discretionary decision-making power. By removing discretion from decision making, the bureaucratic ideal eliminates from its functioning the waste and arbitrariness of less rational modes of organising (Gray, 2009). Indeed, '[T]he more the bureaucracy is "dehumanised" the more completely it succeeds in eliminating from official business love, hatred, and all purely personal, irrational and emotional elements which escape calculation. This is the specific nature of bureaucracy and it is appraised as its special value' (Weber, 1946:215–16, cited in Fineman, 2001:219).

This 'ideal' model of organising places emotion in ontological opposition to reason. By requiring impersonal adherence to the rule-bound specificities of an individual's work role, it seeks to eliminate what are seen as the human frailties of prejudice, favouritism and emotional bias, each of which is presumed to prevent the customer obtaining a fair and neutral service (Tijsterman & Overeem, 2008; Gray, 2009). Effectively, feelings are to be pushed beyond the boundaries of organisation (left at the door) in a modernist belief that 'efficiency should not be sullied by the irrationality of personal feelings' (Hancock & Tyler, 2001:130), especially where 'emotions affect your ability to think, communicate and act effectively' (Penn Behavioural Health, 2008:1). From Weber's bureaucratic ideal through Taylor's scientific management (1911) and on to many contemporary accounts of operations management, emotions are positioned as a barrier to effective production, such that scholars and practitioners of organising have 'tended to ignore the role of emotion at work in favour of more "rational" views of our work lives' (Shuler & Sypher, 2000:54). This is particularly true of very strong emotions that are presumed to interfere with daily life, affect perceptions of those involved, and impair routine task performance by distorting rational operating procedures (Thoits, 1985; Morris & Feldman, 1996; Ashforth & Kreiner, 1999; Fineman, 1999). It is for this reason that managers must apparently 'control emotions for better interpersonal relations and more productive results' (Penn Behavioural Health, 2008:1).

This picture of clockwork rationality can hold (if at all) only if workers are not called upon to deal in or with emotions as part of their work. And here is the rub. Emotions are increasingly recognised as something consumers want as part of their service encounters. Within service economies there is growing pressure not just to control emotions as part of the smooth ordering of relations within bureaucracies but also to manage and display emotions as part of the encounter with the outside world.

Rationalised emotions

Emotions started to be written back into mainstream accounts of organising during the late twentieth century as postindustrial economies moved from the production of material things to the delivery of services and experiences. When you sell experiences to customers, they expect to be treated as individuals, as special, as people who should feel good about the experiences on offer. This results in the perceived need to rationalise the emotions of the service encounter. Concepts such as 'emotional intelligence' (Salovey & Mayer, 1990; Goleman, 1996) are forwarded as value-free mental techniques for aligning and improving emotion management so as 'to produce idealized corporate character through the measurement of emotion to allow fine grained disciplining, dividing, ranking, and tracking of improvement, thus constituting a type of control of self' (Clegg & Baumeler, 2010:1722). Moreover, emotions are brought back in to formal organising because 'customers appear to want empathy from service workers, a genuine commitment to giving good service and a feeling that they are being treated as an individual rather than the next customer in the line' (Korczynski, 2001:80). This fairly limited readmittance of emotions sees workers being selected and remunerated according to their ability to offer emotional performances that engender the right state of mind in the consumer (Hochschild, 1983). For example, job descriptions for doctors' receptionists typically include reference to 'excellent communication/interpersonal skills; previous customer service experience' the ability to 'deal in a courteous manner with all queries from patients and outside agencies' and 'empathise with patients . . . to be compassionate and caring' (Shared Care Practice, job description for doctor's receptionist). In this way organisations are now concerned to control the emotions of workers in the name of a better consumer experience.

As certain feelings are let back in as desired or required performances of, say, empathy or cheerfulness or joyful subservience to customer demands, so employees are required to work within the feeling rules of their employing organisation. The worker is required to regulate their emotional responses to the consumer, painting on a smile (Hochschild, 1983), disciplining the self to deliver an interactive script (Clegg & Baumeler, 2010) or buying into the culture, norms and aims of the organisation such that they engage in the type of deep emotional acting that makes feigning unnecessary (Hochschild, 1983). Under such circumstances the useful potential of private feelings is realised through the commodification of emotional labour with a view to maximising customer satisfaction with a service encounter. James, a hotelier, explained this process in terms of the desire to really please people, even when they are unreasonable:

> We bend over backwards; we really do, to please people. We're passionate about it. . . . So we try and deal with people all the same. So, if you think they're being really unreasonable you still kind of force yourself

to deal with them as you deal with anybody else, and it's "the customer is always right" so be as courteous as you can to them.

(James, hotelier and innkeeper)

The bureaucratic organisational ideal thus develops to produce efficient services that meet the affective needs of the consumer through the control of workers physically, mentally and emotionally. Workers learn to respond to the needs of the customer on behalf of an employing organisation, which is transformed into what Korczynski (2001) labels the 'customer-orientated bureaucracy'.

Working with the contradictions of rationalities

The customer-oriented bureaucracy varies from Weber's bureaucratic ideal insofar as the consumer is recognised as a coproducer of the 'experiences' being sold. As coproducer the consumer claims a right to influence how her experiences are produced if she is not to take her business elsewhere. Consequently, it is no longer enough for the organisation to focus solely on its own internal logic of rational authority and productive efficiency (of things, services or emotions). Rather, the emergence of the 'sovereign' consumer requires that the organisation also adapt its structures and workers to the consumer's needs. In short, the need for efficient task completion must now sit alongside and in tension with the requirement to please the consumer (Korczynski, 2001).

For the worker the resulting tension is manifest in the need to respond to two masters: the manager, with her internal focus on the efficient production of standardised services, and the external consumer, who demands an individualised response to his specific desires. Such pressures might be observed in the modern service factory of the 'call centre', where workers must balance the need to meet the consumer's demand for an individualised and possibly time-consuming service with the organisation's demand to process enquiries as quickly as possible in order to minimise costs and maximise throughput. In such cases the worker must live with the potentially dysfunctional outcomes of the competing rationalities of rational systems (see Barker, 1993; Warner, 2007; Tijsterman & Overeem, 2008, for more on this theme).

What Korczynski's (2001) customer-oriented bureaucracy usefully reminds us is that, when emotions are readmitted to organising, the competing rationalities of bureaucratic functioning and customer focus can come into conflict. Where these demands align we might assume that meeting them is unproblematic. Where they do not, they raise systemic tensions that threaten to place the worker in an impossible position between two apparently sovereign powers. When faced with a demanding customer, should the worker smile and bend to the former's every need or heed the competing managerial demand to take the customer's cash and move on? What about those darker encounters where the customer is unreasonable, abusive or violent? How is the worker to react? Is the consumer always king?

In what follows we consider what happens when the consumer is unreasonable or difficult. What is the response of the frontline service worker when the demands and deeds of the customer run counter to the internal imperative for efficient task completion? What is the appropriate affective response of a worker who is aware that the internal rules and goals of the customer-oriented bureaucracy preclude meeting the demand being made by a customer, while forthright opposition to those demands on the part of the worker is precluded by a rhetoric of consumer sovereignty and associated feeling rules? In short, how is the worker to respond when they can neither empathise nor oppose? One answer, rather appropriate in the context of our discussion of bureaucracy, lies in the performance of *emotional neutrality*.

We consider next the ways in which emotional neutrality is employed as a technique used to 'suppress emotions felt whilst displaying unemotional behaviour, wherein the suppression of the emotion is the performance itself' (Ward & McMurray, 2011:1585). We are not concerned here with the performance of neutrality in familial or social contexts where it has 'use value'. We confine ourselves here to those darker occasions on which workers choose to employ such techniques as part of their labour for 'exchange value'. Thus, while we acknowledge that there may be a range of contexts and reasons for performing emotional neutrality, we focus on those that arise from the difficulties of employed work, starting with experiences of abuse.

Finding a response to the contradictions of service work through emotional neutrality

While there is evidence to suggest that dealing with difficult emotional encounters can be a source of job satisfaction and pride (Shuler & Sypher, 2000; Korczynski, 2001; McMurray & Ward, 2014), there is no getting away from the fact that most service workers are at one time or another subjected to customer abuse. Korczynski & Evans (2013:769) define such abuse as 'forms of customer behaviour which are seen by service workers as aggressive, intimidating or insulting to themselves'. During our research we have witnessed and discussed receptionists being racially abused, car sales staff being attacked, nurses threatened, police and prison officers assaulted, and home care assistants deliberately injured by word and deed. The intensity and complexity of such abusive encounters is usefully illustrated by James's recollection of an unpleasant encounter with a hotel guest. The extract is represented here in detail to give a sense of the interplay of emotions, motivations, service contradictions and effects:[1]

> So there was an incident a wee while ago where, he was an arsehole this guy, he really was a dickhead. They asked for Room One on the

booking with Late Rooms [a booking website], but I missed that detail on the request. I got a call from the staff saying they've arrived [the guests] but they're really not happy, they wanted Room One.

So I said they could have had it but we'd had a leak, it's not leaking now, but needed cleaning. So I said 'clean bloody Room One'.

We bent over backwards, they'd asked for it, so we got the cleaner in and I personally cleaned everything up, everything sparkly again, so we moved them into Room One and moved the booking for the next day.

The next day it leaked in Room One again from the shower in the room above. So the wife came through and said:

'James, oh there's water coming through!' so I went through to Room One.

Now, earlier that night he'd [the husband] been into the bar with his dog – big bloody dog – and let it off the lead. There was a band playing and he was just letting the dog wander through the pub. So the chef, he said to him quite politely 'sorry sir, this is the dog friendly area over here, if you can keep your dog in here, because people are eating'. I think this rubbed him up the wrong way.

Anyway, I went into Room One and he [the husband] was pissed drunk; I thought he was going to punch me; he shouted and swore at me:

'Is This What You Fucking Expect From A Four Star Fucking Hotel, Would You Fucking Stay Here.'

I was literally shaking after the affair. Honestly, I mean yes, there was water dripping, and I said,

'I can move you to different room right now.'

[Customer] 'We Want This Fucking Room, We Wanted This Fucking Room, Would You Fucking Stay Here' – every other word was an F – 'Look At That Fucking Blind, Look At That Fucking Blind, I Can't Sleep With That Fucking Blind With Light Coming In'.

He was mortal drunk, so I thought, right, we'll try and deal with him as we deal with anyone, he is unreasonable but there is a reason to complain. He could have just said he was not happy and that the blind was bothering him and that some water had come in. Initially I said:

'Listen sir I am really sorry, there is nothing much I can do with that right now, I can move you into another room right now.'

He replied 'I Can't Go To The Fucking Toilet, I Can't Turn The Fucking Lights On [because of the water leak].'

I said 'I can move you to another room straight away. Obviously we won't charge you for tonight. You can stay for free and there is breakfast.'

[Customer] 'Its Fucking Midnight, Its Fucking 12 O'clock At Night, I Don't Want To.'

You put your bloody heart and soul into this place. You break your back to keep people happy, and your [*sic*] passionate about it, and you want to make it a success and if you don't your [sic] out of a job and all the rest of it, so, the emotions get up a little bit – but I try to stay calm.

I say again, 'I can move you into this room for free.'

Customer: 'I Don't Care About The Money, I'm Fucking Loaded.'

And his wife, this poor lady, is bright red and embarrassed. And I thought, this guy is a dickhead.

In the end I said you can leave if you want to sir. He just wanted to shout at me. He just wanted to release the anger that had built up from being told he could not walk his dog in the pub.

(James, hotelier and innkeeper)

The account offered by James is suffused with emotion. There is the initial irritation at having to repair and prepare a preferred room (So I said 'clean bloody Room One') – an inefficient act that requires the deployment of cleaning staff to meet a consumer demand. There is the violence of the customer's complaint ('Would You Fucking Stay Here'), the suppressed violence of James's feelings ('this guy is a dickhead'), the long-term passion for the business ('you break your back to keep people happy, and your [sic] passionate about it'), the management of self ('I try to stay calm') as well as the secondary emotions that arise from retelling the tale and verbalising outward expressions and internal reflections. James tolerates the abuse within the context of the demands of a customer-orientated bureaucracy. In this case the presumptions and frustrations of the sovereign consumer build over time as limits placed on the roaming of the customer's dog and dissatisfaction with the room erupt in a violent verbal outburst. James is caught in what others have described as the tension between organisational drives to be 'efficient and competitive' and 'meeting the consumer's desire for satisfaction' (Bunting, 2004:70). As Bunting goes on to note, '[B]alancing the two is no mean feat, given the often unrealistic promise of consumer culture that "we can have whatever we want whenever we want it" ' with the result that 'the failure to cope with this tension is placed on the shoulders of the individual employee, rather than acknowledged as a contradiction of the position they've been placed in' (Bunting, 2004:70). And it is not just in the private sector that the rigidities of structures are felt to be in opposition to notions of consumer sovereignty.

In England's publicly funded National Health Service, doctors' receptionists are faced with the imposed rigidities of: limited numbers of appointment slots, strict criteria for filling slots, and limited frontline discretion to change or allocate slots (all classic features of a bureaucracy as applied to lower-level workers). In addition, they are faced with patients who are increasingly encouraged to act as sovereign consumers who expect flexible appointment slots at short notice and at times convenient to them. Under such circumstances frustration arises for customer and worker alike at not being able to deliver/experience the type and level of service required to enchant the consumer. The worker has limited discretion and the patient little or no choice. Consumers suffer the realisation that 'their expectations of being sovereign are an illusion' (Brook, 2007:366). The worker can, as described here in respect of Gabby, suffer the fallout of that realisation. For Gabby, the failure to fulfil the enchanted myth of the sovereign consumer resulted in her being racially abused by a patient who could not be given an immediate appointment slot:

> The patient came in . . . and she was talking to another receptionist and she was really annoyed with me because I'd made her the appointment on Monday and I didn't give her the appointment straight away. I don't think she understood the whole situation. So when I got to the front desk the patient was shouting and swearing and she'd been racist to me . . . she told me she was going to hit me with her stick and . . . it was ridiculous . . . and it were awful . . . even after Heather had spoken to her she was still saying things and . . . she was in reception and she was talking to other patients and still saying racist things. . . . Even though we told her many times to calm down she just carried on and she was pointing and reaching towards me.
>
> (Gabby, doctor's receptionist).

Despite being racially assaulted in front of colleagues and other patients, Gabby remained calm and attempted to reason with the irate patient. When asked why she had reacted in this way, she highlighted an important distinction between how she chose to behave at work and how she would have behaved outside the organisational context:

> Just because I know it's my job. I just know that I can't. . . . It's funny because at home I would shout back straight away and then I'd think 'Oh I've done the right thing, I've put them in their place!' but at work it made me see that when you shout like that it doesn't get you anywhere and I'd just look as silly as she did.
>
> (Gabby, doctor's receptionist)

In the same way that organisational rules and norms control Gabby's physical labour (e.g. physical presence and presentation, use of time, task selection), they also prescribe her emotional displays and performances in the form of emotional labour (Morris & Feldman, 1996). She constrains her feelings for the good of the organisation and herself, offering instead an emotional performance she does not feel. We know it is a performance because Gabby did not 'shout back' and 'put them in their place' as she would have at home. Instead she, just like James (the hotelier) before her, performed what we have identified elsewhere (Ward & McMurray, 2011) as *emotional neutrality*.

What Gabby is describing is a situation in which it is inappropriate to perform positive or negative emotional labour or let her genuine emotions show through. Instead, she performs *emotional neutrality*. Schuler and Sypher (2000) offer a very broad definition of emotional neutrality insofar as they see it as a communicative accomplishment displaying neither anger nor humour. Morris and Feldman (1996:991) go a little further, noting that 'display rules emphasizing emotional neutrality are used to convey dispassionate authority and status'. Rachel, an HR director, offers an example:

> When you have a member of staff who is pinching out of the till and I'm doing an investigation and disciplinary situation with them, it is just very matter-of-fact, but it's still not unkind, because obviously they are very emotional in a situation like that, and I'll say 'can I get you a glass of water, take your time' and I'm very good with them. I wouldn't be nice because it's not that situation and we need to be serious and matter of fact, but that's as far as it would go.
>
> (Rachel, HR director)

For Rachel, neutrality is expressed as being 'matter-of-fact'. She is aware that the emotions of the 'other' may be heightened, so her emotional performance is designed to be dispassionate in the context of an issue that prescribes that she cannot be 'unkind' or 'nice'. The 'matter-of-fact' performance speaks to her enactment of a bureaucratic role, retold through the language of rationality, in which she has the authority to enforce rules that determine the future of others. In this example the 'other' is an employee rather than a customer, though for Rachel the line is in some senses blurred insofar as she may be called on to discipline, assist, comfort or help employees in respect of certain wants and needs, in much the same way as when dealing with external customers. She uses the same kind of neutrality when dealing with 'difficult customers' in the retail sector. Moreover she also trains her staff on how to:

> handle difficult customers, when customers are shouting and things . . . so you're not being overly nice but your not saying 'don't ruddy talk to me like that' because you can't say that.
>
> (Rachel, HR director)

Here again, reference to the fact that 'you can't say that' speaks to the context of the emotional encounter. It speaks to the manner in which the myth of consumer sovereignty frames feeling rules such that the 'standards used in emotional conversations to determine what is rightly owed and owing in the currency of feeling' (Hochschild, 1989:18) is skewed in favour of the customer. It is the customer who gives free rein to their feelings while workers must labour to control their emotional display and in so doing defuse or cope with difficult and abusive encounters.

It is important to recognise that the presentation of emotional neutrality is in fact a performance. By its very nature, emotional neutrality is difficult to observe given that such displays are intended to convey the absence of feeling on the part of the worker. To observe emotional neutrality one must get below the surface of the performance – to invite the worker to verbalise whether and, if so, how his or her inner feelings varied from his outward presentation. Returning to James's account of the abusive guest, we can see how his performance of neutrality masked deep feelings of frustration and anger:

> James: But honestly I was literally shaking afterwards with fucking anger. What I would really liked to have done is take his suitcases, throw them out of the door and, if I could of – he was a big guy – I'd have nutted [headbutted] him. I would have told him to fuck off and not come back to the hotel. I don't care what he would have written on TripAdvisor. You don't have to take that shit from people. Yes, if there is a problem somebody can come and speak to you. Be reasonable about things. I had a solution for him! I didn't know water was going to come through – it was a little dribble, it wasn't a pipe burst.
> Robert: You say you don't have to take it, but pretty much you did?
> James: It's knowing what happened to this place in the past. It takes a long time to build up a name and a short time to ruin it. . . . You don't want to have conflict with people. You take pleasure in people leaving and saying they had a good time. A lot of people we get come back are almost friends. But you'll always get dickheads.
>
> (James, hotelier and innkeeper)

Effectively it transpires that James does have to take it. Fearful of loss of reputation and the loss of business that this might incur in the 'TripAdvisor age', he suppresses his 'fucking anger' and takes the 'shit' from the customer. For the sake of the business he enacts *emotional neutrality*: 'a technique used to suppress emotions felt whilst displaying unemotional behaviour, wherein the suppression of the emotion is the performance itself' (Ward & McMurray, 2011:1585). In similar vain Bunting (2004:66) notes, for call centre workers, 'If a customer is difficult or rude, the call handler must not respond aggressively. He or she certainly can not betray any irritation or frustration', either during the encounter in question or in the next call that is immediately routed through; instead, 'they must continually repress their own emotions to ensure a standardised service'.

Such performances of emotional neutrality fit with the outward presentation of rationalised organising and authority. They recall the Weberian archetype of an efficient and calculated service from which the presumed bias of emotion appears to have been removed. Of course, emotion is not removed but rather denied. The aggression or the vulgarity of the client is ignored while the feelings of the worker are suppressed. Moreover, such suppression often 'requires a lot of effort' (Shuler & Sypher, 2000:64). As Adam, a prison officer, notes:

> The hardest thing will probably be keeping hold of your emotions when people are trying to goad you and get a reaction out of you. . . . I try to

keep my voice level and calm – keep my voice at a stage where I am not raising it and not escalating [the situation].

(Adam, prison officer)

Given that such performances require effort, it is important to understand why workers perform emotional neutrality and how they make sense of such service encounters.

Making sense of emotional neutrality

We have established that, when faced with the abuse that flows from the contradictions inherent in the customer-orientated bureaucracy, workers can be found performing emotional neutrality. We have also seen that they perform such labour to stay within feeling rules, to prevent the complete violation of the myth of consumer sovereignty and for the maintenance of business reputations. It is also associated with survival, control and care.

Performing neutrality for survival

Staying within the rules can be a matter of organisational survival for the labourer. The call centre worker, the receptionist and the waiter all live with the suspicion that to shout back at a rude customer is to risk a subsequent complaint and even disciplinary procedures. Under such circumstances they must perform emotional neutrality. Moreover, some workers understand that neutrality is required even where verbal assaults escalate into physical violence. As Laura and Vera recount, failure to control one's emotions and acts in the face of such violence can lead to the dismissal of the worker:

> Laura: As I say, with dementia they can be quite violent or aggressive, it's no point you arguing, you just walk away.
> Vera: You need patience.
> Laura: You have got to have an awful lot of patience and walk away for your own sake. Because sometimes you could get so angry with somebody that, that it might be automatic to lash out. And a friend of mine got the sack for it and I was so sorry, so sorry she went, because she [the client] was a nasty old women. I am not condoning it [the lashing out] you don't hold a grudge. If they are nasty or anything it's forgot, it's gone, like they forget you.
> (Laura and Vera, home care workers)

Here, then, it is made clear that the performance of neutrality – of not giving vent to feelings – can be a matter of keeping your job ('for your own sake'). The same applies to the Samaritan, the police officer, the airline cabin crew and myriad other frontline workers who know that the failure to maintain emotional restraint can cost them their job. In each case, worker resistance to a customer's claim is likely to be experienced as an affront to the notion of 'consumer sovereignty' (Korczynski & Ott, 2004). Workers are required to engage in self-surveillance and self-control if they are to avoid sanction. At the root of such control of self is the perceived or actual surveillance of others. Steve made this very point in respect of the surveillance he perceived that he was under in his role as a serving police officer:

> You have lots of things going round your head when you talk to people. You have your professionalism as a person. I'm a big one for doing the right thing. I will do the right thing: simple as! Erm, but it comes into conflict sometimes with what the police want me to do, it comes into conflict with what the victims might want you to do; but as long as I can stay true to myself, then I'm quite happy. . . . The police try and tell you all the while you are working for the victims, you are working for the community and all these sorts of things. But in the background you know that they are always watching and they're quite happy to jump on you straightaway.
>
> (Steve, police officer)

While Steve doesn't mention neutrality specifically (the extract is part of a wider discussion of the need to be professional and to present the appropriate face), he raises, once again, the 'conflict' between the demands of the bureaucracy and the wants of the client. Steve tries to make sense of this in terms of being 'true to myself' and doing 'the right thing'. However, this is accompanied by the perception that others ('the police') are 'always watching' and 'happy to jump on you'. In this sense the maintenance of neutrality becomes an issue of control.

Emotional neutrality and control

Steve is not alone in his suspicion that his ability to offer the correct emotional performances is surveyed by other organisational members. Volunteers at Samaritans (a charity dealing with emotional well-being and suicide) are made aware that their failure to produce the appropriate emotional displays of empathy or neutrality could and should lead to them being reported by a coworker to their branch director. The aim is to maintain the organisational commitment to nonjudgemental listening whether the caller is suicidal, lonely, confused or a self-confessed paedophile. The effect is to subject the worker to a regime of emotional control. Although this is intended for the well-being of both the client and the worker, the costs associated with submission to such regimes fall most heavily on the latter. Judged by customers, coworkers and managers through the apparatus of the employing bureaucracy, the worker is subjected to a spatial ' "nesting" of hierarchized surveillance' dedicated in part to supervision, constraint and even punishment (Foucault 1977/1991:172). It becomes clear to the employee that for the most part 'expressions of fear, anger or anxiety, and other disruptive emotions, are not acceptable' (Clegg & Baumeler, 2010:1725). In this sense, workers may perform emotional neutrality because they are compelled to do so by the apparatus of and contradictions inherent in service-orientated bureaucracies. At one level, then, emotional neutrality arises as an effect of control.

Of course, it is in the nature of emotional labour that workers are simultaneously subject to and contribute towards the norms and environments that require certain types of performances. To the extent that workers comply with the need to survey self and other, they reinforce the need for specific emotional performances. Indeed, it may the case that workers value the control that performances of emotional neutrality promise, as described by Adam, the prison officer:

> It's all about de-escalation. If you can resolve a situation by talking rather than laying hands-on, then let's resolve it that way. . . . You try to bring a situation down, it's best for us and its best for them [agitated prisoners]. . . . It's all about safety. . . . People have this idea about prison being a dangerous place, and don't get me wrong it can be – there's been members of staff stabbed quite badly in recent years and there's a lot of people in there [prison] who are dangerous people, you mustn't loose [*sic*] sight of that – but you build relations. You can control people to a degree by siting [*sic*] down and talking to them. We're not talking about being pally, but having a professional 'us' and 'them' relationship. I think that helps to control the environment.
>
> (Adam, prison officer)

Within the context of prison work, neutrality is performed and valued for its potential to de-escalate a situation. It is performed as part of a process intended to manage difficult situations in which the worker seeks to maintain control. Prison officers are not interested in being friends or 'pally' with prisons, but they are aware that having amiable relations can ease their own working day insofar as it mitigates violence or related difficulties. De-escalation through the performance of neutrality is preferable to the use of aggression and physical force insofar as the latter not only threaten the safety of the worker but also require additional work in terms of form filling and enquiries in the aftermath of physical (rather than emotional) prisoner constraint.

It might be objected that such a concern with control is a consequence of the extremes of the prison environment. While this is in part true, the importance of control is also not lost on those in more 'regular' organisational environs:

> So I think it is sometimes how you handle it [conflict]. If you're in control of your emotions and you can handle it, then you can diffuse those situations a lot better.
>
> (Rachel, HR director)

Emotional neutrality makes sense where it is both an effect of and an instrument in the control of self and others. It may be performed in order to safeguard one's position or to seek control over a given situation as part of one's organisational role. It can also be offered as a form of care.

Emotional neutrality as care

While control is a major feature of the performance of emotional neutrality, there may be other factors that make sense of such labour. For example, our work with Samaritans, nurses, receptionists, vets and care workers points to the performance of neutrality as an act of care and understanding. Two examples will suffice to make the point. In the first, from a home carer, neutrality is offered in the face of personal harm:

> Jenny: I loved that job I really did. But it could be dangerous. There was a big fella who we knew could be aggressive and I said to him, 'you're not going to hit me are you' but he did, right in the face. I woke up looking at the ceiling thinking 'what am I doing down here'. Then there was the woman who would scratch you. She would demand that you come closer saying that she could not hear, and once you were right in, she would swipe you across the face.
> Robert: What did you do?
> Jenny: You do nothing. You walk away. It doesn't matter how you feel, they're not well so you do nothing. It could be upsetting. Sometimes I would go home in a terrible state.
> (Jenny, former home care worker)

Neutrality here presents as to 'do nothing' and 'walk away'. Poorly paid and subject to physical abuse, such carers learn that it 'doesn't matter how you feel' – the expected response is a neutral one. In part this neutrality is offered in acknowledgement that clients aren't well. In the same way that GP receptionists excuse abusive patients on the basis that they are ill, fearful or scared in respect of their own ill health (Ward & McMurray, 2011), home carers make sense of unpleasant encounters and neutral responses through reference to the condition of the client (Johnson, 2015). Similarly, while Samaritans mostly respond to the emotional woes of others with empathy, occasionally they take calls from people whose thoughts or deeds they cannot condone (most notably, if rarely, paedophiles) but in respect of whom they will listen with neutrality in the hope that such care might lead the caller to reflect on his acts.

Such acts of care can offer a sense of reward to both the carer and the client. It can also be a rewarding part of the work role insofar as workers successful deploy the emotional skills in which they have been trained (Shuler & Sypher, 2000; McMurray & Ward, 2014). It can also overlap with the need for control, as described in the protection of a child:

> [I] know how to stay calm and that obviously is an act. When you're restraining a child at the top of a set of stairs – that was a couple of

months ago – I'm not calm, but that is what they [the children] see, they think I am, so they stay calm.

(Hannah, primary school teacher)

Here, as in most of the cases we have considered, the performance of neutrality speaks to the presentation of a particular image. For better or worse, it says something about the worker. It speaks to the effects of performing emotional neutrality on both the worker and those around them as the worker seeks to engender the right frame of mind in others. In this case the 'other' is not just the child at the top of the stairs but also the other children watching. The performance of neutrality has a wider audience than the immediate consumer. It is offered as part of an attempt to communicate what is expected in a given organisational context and of a particular occupational role. It speaks to a disciplining and presentation of self as part of wider regimes of control, surveillance and care.

Finally, it is worth noting that the performance of emotional neutrality has a range of identity consequences for workers. To the extent that neutrality conveys 'dispassionate authority and status' (Morris & Feldman, 1996:991), it might be valued as an important part of identity construction, as in the emotional detachment that has long spoken to the professionalism of medics (Bunting, 2004) or the impartiality of the HR director, the incorruptibility of the police officer or the resilience of the prison guard. For others the consequences are more negative. Our work with GP receptionists found that emotional neutrality was often read by patients as an absence of care, excess bureaucracy and even malevolence (Ward & McMurray, 2011). This gives rise to the stereotype of the doctor's receptionist as the 'dragon behind the desk' (Arber & Sawyer, 1985).

What advice is there for coping with the identity consequences of performing emotional neutrality? Rachel, the HR manager, tells herself and her employees

not to take it personally. Because I know it's not always me. In my personal life I am a very sensitive person. If we were friends and I thought I had upset you I'd be devastated, but in a work situation I know it's not me if I'm being shouted at, they're just venting their spleen and that's fine . . . it's just how you handle that.

(Rachel, HR director)

This process of not taking it personally is not always easy. As Jack, a veterinarian, revealed in his discussion of the 'dark side of euthanasia' and the aggression of owners:

you've got to realise that actually the only reason they're being aggressive is because they're emotionally attached and they're not in control of those emotions, and so it's just letting them voice their opinions, get their emotion out, and then talking to them. But, yes, that, that will often eat me when I go home . . . [but] . . . then I can cope with that side of it because I know I'm doing it for the animal and at the end of the day I'm stopping the animal suffering.

(Jack, veterinarian)

This brings us back to where we began, namely the idea that emotional neutrality speaks to emotional performances in particular organisational contexts. Those contexts simultaneously require the performance of emotional neutrality on the part of the worker and enable the worker to make sense of such performances, whether in terms of being subjected to control, seeking control themselves, offering care, deploying learned skills, presenting a professional image or negotiating the contradictions inherent in customer-oriented bureaucracies. For most, the performance of emotional neutrality arises from and speaks to a combination of factors. It may be a source of frustration and / or pride. For better or worse, these performances also inform our images of particular individuals, occupations, professions and organisations.

Conclusions

Our argument in this chapter is that the inability to observe emotions should not be taken to imply their absence. Where overt displays of care, love, joy, frustration or anger can not be identified it does not necessarily mean that organising is taking place in an emotional vacuum. On the contrary, the appearance and maintenance of a Weberian rational ideal is very likely to be founded on a display of emotional neutrality. Under such conditions the suppression of feelings and the presentation of a dispassionate face *is* the emotional performance. It speaks to concerted efforts to control that which is felt in order to resist or modify the performance of another. It speaks to performances that enact what it means to organise in a given context, such that emotional labour becomes 'part of the very structure of organization' (Shuler & Sypher, 2000:81).

Often such performances are evoked in the face of negative emotions from others (clients, colleagues, superiors), at times when to vent one's true feelings would be deemed unacceptable organisationally and/ or risk sanction personally. They speak to contexts in which the performance of empathy or antipathy is inappropriate, while the option of exiting the scene is either rejected or unavailable. The response offered instead is that of emotional neutrality. It speaks to the necessary improvisation described by Clegg & Baumeler (2010:1728) in which 'individuals must act, plan actions and calculate the likely gains and losses of acting (or failing to act) under conditions of endemic uncertainty'. The position is uncertain because to acquiesce to unreasonable consumer demands risks overburdening the organisation with prohibitive costs and obligations, not to mention potentially demeaning oneself, while resisting the consumer goes against the rationality of the consumer-orientated bureaucracy and risks the combined wrath of customer and employer.

When performed well, neutrality presents as a matter-of-fact statement of rules, positions, options or actions. It may mask empathy, as in the case of the receptionist who, while understanding that a patient's verbal violence is a consequence of fear or pain, can not be seen to condone such outbursts. Alternatively, it may mask the anger felt by the police officer who, while being subjected to verbal and physical violence, must be seen to respond with dispassionate professionalism and restraint. In both these contexts, neutrality is performed in order to stay within the operating and display rules of the employing organisation. At one level the performance of emotional neutrality speaks to the triumph of rational authority and bureaucratic control as feelings are masked and emotions performed in the service of organisational aims through Foucauldian practices of self-surveillance. Considered thus, emotional encounters appear as 'sites of darkness' (Warner, 2007:1023) in which the iron cage of rationality governs the very presentation of self.

At another level, the performance of neutrality might be examined as part of an organisational or personal process designed to explain and thus cope with the behaviour of others. Again we see this in the receptionist's recourse to explaining patient behaviour in terms of fear or pain or in Rachel's ability to compartmentalise the shouting of others as an expressive venting of general frustration rather than as a personal attack. The positioning of another's emotions as 'nothing personal' has the effect of partially removing the worker from the firing line. The unwanted emotions or actions of others are framed/rationalised as directed at the context, situation or role occupied by the labourer rather than at the worker personally. This enables the worker to make sense of the encounter as one which necessitates and invites an 'organisational' rather than personal performance and response. Neutrality may therefore be offered as an organisationally appropriate performance in which the actions of others are neither condoned nor condemned in emotional terms. On a personal level the performance of neutrality may be made easier by the belief that an unwanted encounter is 'nothing personal', thus reducing the gap between feelings and display.

The performance of neutrality is not without its problems. It may be taken as a sign of being a hard, uncaring or even callous service provider. It evokes negative associations with inflexible bureaucracy and unfeeling bureaucrats. There may also be costs for the labourer, not only the negative identity consequences for the occupation, but also the burden of retaining an indifferent mask or backgrounding one's self in favour of the maintenance of a role. Such burdens arise because the performance of emotional neutrality requires that the worker mask his or her true feelings and modify his emotional performances such that he gives the appearance of rational neutrality. What we can be certain of is that 'emotion and rationality are intertwined, and there is a lot about emotion and emotional labour that is rational' (Shuler &

Sypher, 2000:85). It behooves us as people, workers, managers and academics to recognise this interrelation and all it implies in terms of skills, costs, rewards, responsibilities and organising.

Note

1 In using this extended extract of text we follow Atkinson (1995) in his assertion that there are times when there is a need to preserve talk in its extended state to appreciate the manner in which an interaction unfolds.

4 Dealing in emotional dirty work

'But my dad, I couldn't tell him what I did because he thought it disgusting. I used to talk to my mum, and he would be listening and he used to think it was disgusting that a young girl – I was only 21 – was doing this for, as he called 'em "dirty old people, dirty old people". Some people can do it and some people can't.'

(Vera, home care worker)

Many of us are required to work with dirt. Indeed, Hughes (1958) contends that most occupations have their dirty work: those physical, social or moral tasks that threaten to soil our lives and stain our identities. Work might be considered dirty because, as in Vera's case, it requires that an individual toil with the urine, faeces, confusion and violence of elderly people needing home care. Alternatively, it might be dirty because it implicates workers in activities or contexts that are deemed sinful, as in the case of Tyler's (2012) sex shop workers. In all such cases, to undertake dirty work is to risk being tainted by such work, so that the worker is seen as 'spoiled, blemished, devalued, or flawed to various degrees' as a consequence of the stigma that arises from their labour (Kreiner *et al.*, 2006:621). Dirty work can also be an emotional experience. For workers it may be a source of self-pride, evoke personal distress, or call forth gallows humour as a mechanism for coping with dirt and taint (Ackroyd & Crowdy, 1990; Jervis, 2001). For those outside, looking in at the worker, it might also evoke repulsion and disgust on the part of those who would seek to avoid being contaminated by dirt. Dirty work is, then, emotional work, but we want to consider whether work *with* emotions can itself be dirty. Specifically, what might it mean to engage in *emotional dirty work*?

So far in this book we have considered what it means to be an emotional labourer in terms of the effects of empathetic performances, the call to antipathetic labour and the presentation of emotional neutrality. Central to these considerations has been the 'type' of performance offered by the worker in respect of clients. In this chapter the focus shifts from the style of emotional offering to particular contexts in which emotional labour requires handling the burdensome, unwanted or dirty emotions of others.

We start by defining what we mean by dirt. Drawing on the work of Hughes (1951, 1958, 1962) and Ashforth and Kreiner (1999) we consider how dirty work has traditionally been thought of in terms of those physical, social and moral tasks that most of us would rather not undertake – tasks which the fortunate among us outsource to others so that we might avoid being contaminated by associations with dirt. A review of the extant literature reveals that this dirty work is often necessary work, enacted on the dark underbelly of organisations where the detritus of everyday living is tidied away. It also becomes clear that, until very recently, emotion has been a marginal factor in the study of dirty work. It was either not considered or seen as a by-product of other forms of dirt and so not explicitly addressed and conceptualised. Building on the first explicit definition of emotional dirt (see McMurray & Ward, 2014), we argue that emotional dirty work speaks to a distinct form of tainted labour. Moreover, we contend that it is a growing feature of employment in secondary and tertiary employment sectors. We illustrate the nature, extent and spread of such work through interview extracts with those engaged in home care, banking, policing, veterinary medicine, reception work and with Samaritans. We start by defining what we mean by dirt.

Dirt as a social construct

To speak of dirt is to speak of a process of delineation in which the clean and worthwhile are separated from the dirty and worthless. It describes a social process of meaning production through which certain ideas, objects or groups are labelled as pollutants or 'things recognisably out of place, a threat to good order' (Douglas, 1966:160). Dirt is in its simplest form 'matter out of place' (Douglas, 1966:35). It is something that does not belong, challenges or disrupts a cherished order and threatens our sense of solidarity – it refers to that which is 'regarded as objectionable and vigorously brushed away' (Douglas, 1966:160). Mud on carpets, ketchup down a suit tie, or graffiti on a corporate billboard can all stand as examples of physical dirt.

Graffiti reminds us that dirt is also symbolic in nature insofar as it speaks to that which pollutes our preferred conceptions of the world (think of the work of Banksy and his public comments on the ills of capitalism, the hypocrisy of certain conceptions of art, the validity of war – all displayed in prominent places and viewed as vandalism by some and as artistic protests by others). It speaks to 'a set of ordered relations and a contravention of that order. . . . Dirt is the by-product of a systematic ordering and classification of matter, in so far as ordering involves rejection of inappropriate elements' (Douglas, 1966:35). In this sense, dirt is that which is ejected and rejected as a consequence of ordering any system: the waste and pollution of production, the packaging and trash of consumption and the ideas neglected during our processes of sense making. It is that which is no longer of use, no longer wanted, no longer valued. Organisationally we might think of middle-aged middle managers who lose their jobs through delayering and are condemned to the scrap heap or those who fall between the well-ordered hurdles of our education systems and fail to gain the qualifications, work or opportunities required to participate in consumer society – they exist instead at the margins.

Under such conditions, the symbolic and social significance of dirty attributions lie in their ability to separate 'clean us' from 'dirty them'. They speak to a delineating practice through which in-groups are separated from out-groups insofar as the latter are positioned as a threat to the order and solidarity of a community. It is a practice through which communities distinguish the worthwhile, acceptable, clean, pure, orderly, unblemished and good from the worthless, unacceptable, tainted, polluted, chaotic, stigmatised and bad (Selmi, 2012). In this sense 'dirt' or 'dirtiness' is not an essential or concrete phenomenon but rather a status 'created by the differentiating activity of the mind' (Douglas, 1966:161). Dirtiness is to be understood as a 'social construction: it is not inherent in the work itself or the workers but is imputed by people based on necessarily subjective standards of cleanliness and purity' (Ashforth and Kreiner, 1999:415) that evoke some sense of rejection or repugnance. It is this sense of repugnance, coupled with a fear of pollution, which threatens to taint those who are called upon to work with dirt.

The dark taint of dirty work

Dirty work is often seen as repugnant because it requires work with issues, problems, tasks or people we would rather not know about (Hughes, 1958, 1962). The very existence of such dirt reminds us 'that the boundaries that separate vice from virtue, good from evil, pure from polluted are permeable, and worse, necessarily permeable' and that '[t]o our disgust, good is always engaging in unseemly compromises that implicate us' (Miller, 1997, cited in Kreiner *et al.*, 2006:619). To be near the boundary is to risk contamination with dirt. It is for this reason that we employ others to undertake such work on our behalf. Lawyers deal with criminals, housing officers with the homeless, psychiatrists with paedophiles, janitors with household waste, morticians with bodies; each acts as our agent of dirty work, marshaling the boundaries between our clean and ordered lives on the one hand and the undifferentiated mass of dirt from which such order rises on the other. It is these third-party agents – these *dirty workers* – who run the risk of being tainted and stigmatised by their association with matter out of place (Hughes, 1962).

Dirty workers' proximity to dirt – their literal and or symbolic willingness to get their hands dirty – is often seen by the rest of society to mark or *taint* them such that, in Goffman's (1997:73) words, they are perceived to exhibit an 'undesired differentness' that marks them out from polite company and effectively devalues them as people. They possess an undesired quality or association that reduces the prestige or esteem of an occupation (Ashforth and Kreiner, 1999; Hughes, 1958; Mills *et al.*, 2007) such that they are tainted in the eyes of others. Under Hughes's (1958) original formulation, there were assumed to be three forms of taint arising from dirty work: physical, social and moral.

Physical taint arises from association with effluence, grime, death or deleterious and unpleasant working conditions (Ashforth & Kreiner, 1999). Such taint can be read in the work of meat cutters, veterinarians, road sweeps, nurses and janitors (Hughes, 1958; Jervis, 2001; McMurray, 2012; Meara, 1974; Sanders, 2010; Simpson *et al.*, 2011). Vera's work as a home care assistant is a case in point as she 'cleans up' people who have 'soiled themselves' by washing and dressing them before stripping and replacing their bed linen, all the while making sure that, if the client is confused, you 'keep their hands out the way – are you with me? – because if they are all covered in faeces and whatnot you don't want their hands down there' (Vera, home care assistant). Vera's work also brings her into contact with social taint.

Social taint is a consequence of being associated with stigmatised publics and tasks or servility to others. Care of those with HIV/AIDs, social work with deprived communities, and caring for the elderly have all been identified as sites associated with servility and stigma (Ashforth & Kreiner, 1999; Ashforth *et al.*, 2007; Haber *et al.*, 2011; Stannard, 1973). Social taint speaks to work that tends to be undervalued by others, in terms of either the social standing of the labourer or the remuneration that accompanies such work (Stacey, 2005) – as Vera's notes, her pay as a home carer is 'absolute crap'.

Then there is the *moral taint* that arises from proximity to notions of sin, dubious virtue or deception and that has been associated with the work of exotic dancers, abortion clinicians, debt collectors, sex shop workers and, latterly, bankers (see Ashforth and Kreiner, 2002; Chiappetta-Swanson, 2005; Grandy, 2008; Stanley & Mackenzie-Davey, 2012; Tyler, 2012). The case of banking is interesting because it reminds us of the socially constructed and fluid nature of dirty attributions. Where once to be in banking was something to be proud of, since the 2007–2008 financial crisis – and the declamation of banking and bankers as self-serving and corrupt – these besuited denizens of the City of London find themselves part of a morally tainted occupation. And it is not just the high-rolling traders that have become besmirched but also those lesser-paid minions of middle and back-office functions who have been tarred with the same brush. As recounted to us personally by Sam, even to be linked to a bailed-out city bank is to be positioned as morally tainted and dirty:

> It, it was not, it was not a pleasant time. At the beginning of my time with [London Bank – pseudonym] and my time with previous banks, I'd been proud to say who I worked for. You don't necessarily shout about working for London Bank any longer, it's not a popular thing at dinner parties to admit that you work for London Bank. If you do say, then say you don't work for the division that made all the losses. Well actually I do (laughter). It's very hard to hold your head up. I was talking to some people after one of the banking seminars, he was with some girls who worked for a Swiss bank, and they said – facetiously obviously – they said sometimes when they're at dinner parties, if they want to have a better reputation, they lie and say they work for Huntington Life Sciences (laughter).
>
> (Sam, middle-office banking worker)[1]

'Huntington Life Sciences' is a reference to a controversial animal research centre, comparison with which is intended to illustrate the stigma that is now attached to a career in banking. To be associated with something lousy, unscrupulous, ineffective and failed (Hughes, 1962) is not 'pleasant'. Indeed, as Ash confided, the moral dirt of banking can taint you in the eyes of family and strangers alike:

> Back home my family were – cos they're not involved [in banking] – they really thought that I was the devil . . . I think they thought I was getting massive bonuses too. . . . Everyone out there that didn't work in banking thought that we were all just getting huge, huge bonuses and it was all our own fault and it serves us right. It wasn't fair . . . everyone was horrible to you on the street.
>
> (Ash, middle-office banking worker)

Sam's and Ash's accounts of moral taint hint at the emotional effects of dirty attributions. To be associated with dirt is 'not pleasant', is even 'horrible'. This chimes with the generalised assumption that physical, social and moral dirty work is by definition unpleasant work (Bergman & Chalkley, 2007; Haber *et al.*, 2011; Jervis, 2001). It should be noted, however, that this is not always the case.

There is a growing literature dedicated to illustrating the ways in which dirty work can be a source of emotional pride, strength and belonging (Ashforth & Kreiner, 1999; Kreiner *et al.*, 2006). In some cases, positive emotional effects run alongside the engagement with dirt; in others they are a product of having undertaken the work itself – of being able to stomach it in a way that others can not, whether this is the gore of butchery, the servility and bodily secretions associated with caring for the elderly or the moral implications of tending to mothers after genetic termination (Ackroyd & Crowdy, 1990; Chiappetta-Swanson, 2005).

Whether the accounts of emotions in dirty work are positive or negative, what they have in common is a tendency to treat emotion as a side effect or outcome of physically, socially or morally tainted work. Emotions are seen as a dependent variable that arises from dirty work, rather than the object of study themselves: they speak to the experience of dirt, rather than being studied as 'dirty' in and of themselves (see, for example, Simpson *et al.*, 2011; Chiappetta-Swanson, 2005). We are interested here in those organisational contexts in which emotions themselves are posited as dirt and are worked over by labourers.

Emotional dirty work

McMurray and Ward (2014:12 [original emphasis]) define emotional dirty work as that which involves handling '*expressed feelings that threaten the solidarity, self-conception or preferred orders of a given individual or community* . . . a subjective state assigned by either the individual involved or outside observers through which emotions are deemed to be in some sense polluting'. Alternatively expressed, it refers to labour with emotions that are deemed out of place, contextually inappropriate, burdensome or taboo. These unwanted feelings may arise from customers, clients or coworkers and require that the worker 'induce or suppress feeling in order to sustain the outward countenance that produces the proper state of mind in others' (Hochschild, 1983:7). An example from one of Vera's fellow home care workers, Laura, usefully illustrates the point.

Working with older people Laura and her colleagues are often the bearers of bad news. The immediate task is one of conveying information, but the more enduring work lies in managing the emotions that result from such information. Here, Laura describes entering a room where an elderly client is crying following the news that her mother has died:

> And I said what's the matter Nelly and Jane said 'oh she has had some bad news Laura, I have just had to tell her that her mum has died and her mum isn't with us any more' . . . and the shock, do you know what I mean. And I said 'oh I am so sorry Nelly' I said 'I am so sorry love'. She was just sat, because no one else was with her, I said 'do you want to come back to your bedroom', 'yes' she said, I said 'come on I will take you back to your bedroom' and I just sat talking to her for five minutes.
> (Laura, home care worker)

Laura identifies with the distress and isolation of the client by making time to guide her to a place of comfort. There is an expression of sympathy ('I am so sorry') and willingness to undertake the emotional work that others appear unwilling or unable to do ('she was just sat, because no one else was with her'). For Laura and Vera such emotional offerings were an important part of the home carer's work. For these labourers the work of a home carer is not just getting people washed and dressed. It is also about tending to the often-neglected emotional needs of clients, whether this requires an emotionally neutral approach to dealing with soiled beds (see Chapter 3), talking through difficult emotions or, as described by Vera here, literally helping a client put on a smile:

> And then I say [to the elderly client] let's put your smile on, and I got on my knees and I put lipstick on [the client] and blot it . . . because that's what she wants.
>
> (Vera, home care worker)

Such work is both socially and emotionally dirty insofar as it implies a level of servility ('I go on my knees') and is directed at repairing an individual's self-concept and sense of order through attention to neglected emotional needs. As observed in other care settings, these acts of servility and empathy also go beyond what is written in workers' job descriptions to gift (Bolton, 2000b) their time and emotions to clients. It is a gift in the sense that there is no direct exchange value, and yet it is conducted within the public realm and in some accord with organisational practices. Vera and Laura effectively work beyond their allotted and paid fifteen minutes to do the dirty work that speaks to the relations between people. It is, however, a gift that not everyone appears able or willing to give:

> some girls, foreign girls and English girls, I have worked with over the years they lack empathy. They can't put themselves in that person's position and feel what that person must be feeling.
>
> (Vera, home care worker)

This type of emotional support (and its avoidance) can also be read in the work of Chiappetta-Swanson's (2005) nurses, who clean up the physical and emotional dirt of genetic termination for fetal anomaly. Where doctors and genetic counsellors avoided the difficult discussions and feelings that accompanied the termination of fetuses with genetic abnormalities, nurses attended to the emotional needs of women with a view to giving 'a sense of emotional control, providing reassurance and support creating emotional attachment' (Chiappetta-Swanson, 2005:108). Like many agents of dirty work, they were forced by their employment to engage with dirt (Jervis, 2001) insofar as nurses (unlike doctors) could not absent themselves from contact with difficult emotions on moral grounds. Dirty emotional work was cast off and handed down the occupational hierarchy, as is so often the case with dirt (McMurray, 2012). And yet, while most nurses reported feeling that such intense involvement with patients was unavoidable, they also deemed it desirable. This included being prepared to 'share their patients' suffering and to cry right along with them' because '[T]his emotional attachment represented for many what nursing was all about, total commitment to caring for one's patient' (Chiappetta-Swanson's, 2005:109–10).

Where the work of genetic-termination nurses speaks to what are likely to be one-off relational encounters, the emotional dirty work of the home care assistant can be more recursive in character. As consider here, the dirty work of empathetic listening is complicated by the client's mental state. Dementia means that the bad news is forgotten and must be redelivered, re-endured and managed time and time again, a point Laura makes in respect of telling Nelly about her mother's death:

> In five minutes she has forgotten it [that her mother has died], and she will ask you the same question. Now, their argument [Laura's employer] was you tell them the truth, but why should she have to relive the sorrow and the grief and go all through that emotion when a little white lie means she is fine. All right, she will ask you the same question again, but it's knowing the person, I would never say that to Nelly never [i.e. that her mother is dead].
>
> (Laura, home care worker)

In this context, dealing with emotionally burdensome interactions becomes an unwanted recursive task for the worker. For Laura, the unpleasant and apparently futile nature of such emotional dirty work suggests the need for recourse to an alternative strategy. By effectively lying to the client, Laura is implicated in a form of moral dirty work insofar as she labours to deceive the client. Faced with a moment of undecidability (McMurray *et al.*, 2011) in which organisational prescriptions for truthful dealing clash with her own desire to tend to the emotional state of the client, she makes the decision to deceive as part of what might be described as personal ethic of care. Interestingly, Chiappetta-Swanson (2005) notes that one of the benefits of being abandoned to dirty work is that the isolation it affords allows the labourer greater scope to act according to her own occupational judgement.

So emotional dirty work involves dealing with the difficult, disruptive and out-of-place emotions of others as part of a work-based encounter. It is work that others would rather avoid for fear that intense and difficult emotions might touch or taint them. It is also work that demands a performative response on the part of the labourer, for example, the empathy or neutrality of home carer or nurse.

Given the examples used thus far, we might begin to suspect that emotional dirty work applies only to those individuals explicitly employed in the public or private provision of health and social services. This is not the case. The need to engage with emotions that are burdensome, polluting or out of place can also be observed in work more usually associated with antipathetic and neutral emotional performances. To illustrate the point, we turn to the work of policing.

Speaking to an occupational similarity that spans the work of home caring and policing, Steve, a long-serving uniformed police officer in the UK, describes the unwanted emotional labour of informing families of the death of a loved one:

> We don't just have to deal with crime, we deal with other things as well, so with regard to say an accident, somebody has died, you've got to give a death message. Now I've never had to give one, and touch wood [colloquialism denoting a wish for good fortune] I don't want to. Because I don't want to stand there and tell somebody that one of their loved ones has died. I don't know, how do you do that? I've got fifteen years [experience] and I still don't know how we do it. I'd like to think I'd be professional and I'd be empathetic but not too empathetic – even down to little things like remembering to keep your hat on.
>
> (Steve, police officer)

The work is emotionally dirty because it is something Steve hopes never to have to do. This burdensome task irrevocably disrupts the preferred order of the recipient's family life and in so doing demands the police officer respond with the appropriate emotional performance: 'empathetic but not too empathetic'. Just like genetic-termination nurses and home carers, police officers are called upon to work with difficult and burdensome emotions that may be shunned by others. They must make a judgement as to the depth and nature of the emotional engagement in respect of clients whose emotional needs demand a response: demand the offer of emotional care. As considered in the next section, this is a complex relational task contingent on material circumstances and an assessment of the needs and character of different members of the public.

Physically, social, morally and emotionally dirty work

Emotional dirty work often overlaps with other forms of dirt. For nurses and home care workers we have seen how emotional dirty work accompanies or even implicates the labourer in morally dirty work. For them, as for police officer Steve, emotional dirt can also coincide with physical dirt. (It should be noted that some readers may find the following extract harrowing. It is included for the sake of completeness, so that we might acknowledge and attend to some of the darkest tasks that we demand of our organised agents of dirty work. It speaks to horrors of physical dirt and the shifting complexity of emotional dirt.) In this case, Steve describes the mechanics, matter and emotions of dealing with a sudden death:

> You go to a sudden death, erm, and one of the things you have to do is you have to search the body and all those sort of things. Well, I had never seen a dead body before I joined. When I first joined, my first

sudden death was horrible. Some old chap. It was in the summer, he died in his living room. He was a bit of a hoarder so never went out of the one room. So there's a bucket in the corner where he used to go to the loo and he used to do his number twos on scraps of newspaper from under a table – so it stank. When he slept at night, he had two chairs and he pulled two chairs together end on end. So he was getting in [to the make-shift chair-bed] and he had his arms – you know when you take your top off and you cross your arms to take it off – well he was up to about chest height and died. Well, we went in and that's how he was. Because he'd been there for five days in the hot it was, it was horrible. And the things were growing out of his eyes and something had gone up his arse and those sorts of things. But emotionally wise, then you've got the rela-tives turn up and you're thinking if that was my granddad I would want to know that. So what you've got to do is, is you've got . . . People are crying their eyes out, blokes are normally trying to keep it together and all this. So you've got different types of emotions from different people. Then you've got somebody who's dead behind you. Then you've got to gauge do I go in, do I stay out, what can I tell them . . . its [*sic*]difficult.

(Steve, police officer)

What strikes the officer and reader first is the physical dirt of the life and death of others. We witness grime, effluent, pollution and all kinds of matter out of place with which the police officer must deal. The role of the officer is to impose order on this disorganised mass, to determine if the death is 'suspicious, do I need to get detectives in here because he's been murdered, or literally he's died in his sleep and I can give it a rest' (Steve, police officer). But soon the requirement for physically dirty work is supplanted by the emotional dirty work of dealing with and responding to the expressed feel-ings of relatives. Steve is required to respond to the emotional needs of oth-ers ('people are crying their eyes out, blokes are normally trying to keep it together') both through reference to his own empathetic projection of how he might react if he were in the relative's position ('if that was my grand-dad I would want to know') while acknowledging that 'you've got different types of emotions from different people . . . you've got to gauge [the emo-tional offering]'. Here we get a sense for the fluid and precarious nature of emotional dirty work as compared to dealing with physical matter. There is a need to find the appropriate type and level of emotional performance, a task which Steve acknowledges is 'difficult'.

Emotional dirty work is difficult because it is unpredictable, avoided by others and often marginal to prescribed organisational interests. As with other forms of dirty work, its significance and place often go unrecognised by other stakeholders, including other occupational groups and clients (Sta-cey, 2005). One explanation for this lack of recognition lies in the presump-tion that emotion work is marginal work insofar as it is associated with both women's work and tainted work.

The taints of emotional dirty work

Steve hints at the gendered presumptions that underpin emotional dirt when he refers to 'people' crying their eyes out and 'blokes' who are *normally* trying to keep it together. Such statements speak to an ideological divide in which masculinity and rationality are positioned in opposition to femininity and emotion. Where the former speaks to organisation and mastery of the self, the latter implies abandoning oneself to the free and chaotic reign of everyday feelings. As considered in Chapter 2, it speaks to a division between the rationality of work and the emotions of home in which 'women are ideologically associated with home-making, child-bearing and rearing and men with the workplace' (James, 1992:501).

Constructed thus as women's work, emotions become everyday occurrences to which any unskilled individual can respond. The ability to listen empathetically, offer a shoulder to cry on, or give time to another's feelings are presumed to be activities that anyone can engage in. Stripped of any notion of practice or mastery, such activities 'disappear most often from job descriptions, performance evaluations and salary calculations' (Guy & Newman, 2004:289). They are positioned instead as marginal activities, which are presumed to require minimal skill, often practiced as a gift (Bolton, 2000b) by marginalised (female) workers in lower organisational positions (James, 1992; Sanders, 2010).

In gendered terms, emotional dirty work is thus tainted as a peripheral concern. While the physical labour of making beds and dressing clients is scheduled into the paid work of the home carer and the intellectual work of solving crimes or reconstructing the sequence of events is recorded in official police statistics, in both cases the emotional labour involved in the management of grief remains peripheral, underrecognised and underrewarded. Just as dirt offends against order (Douglas, 1966), so emotion offends classical organisational concerns with rationality. It is a by-product of organising which, as Douglas (1966:40) reminds us in respect of dirt more broadly, 'must not be included if preferred patterns of organisational functioning are to be maintained'. Emotion, as dirt, pollutes the rationalised fiction of well-ordered, controlled and knowable organising and organisations. It breaks down the divides between work and home, public and personal, paid and gifted, masculine and feminine, stable and fluid, organised and chaotic. To work at such margins is to risk being tainted by that which offends against our preferred orders.

Labourers risk being tainted because they are implicated in activities that are judged not to be real work (not core or valued work). Insofar as it requires contact with difficult or burdensome emotions, dirty work is also presumed to be undesirable work, and this presumption is reinforced when individuals avoid such work by passing it down the occupational hierarchy (Chiappetta-Swanson, 2005; McMurray, 2012).

Despite the forced nature of much dirty work, there is often an external presumption of choice on the part of the worker. This gives rise to questions such as 'How can you do it?' (Ashforth & Kreiner, 1999:413) and 'why would you want to do that?' (McMurray & Ward, 2014:13). Under such questioning, the dirty worker is effectively challenged to justify his or her engagement with dirt, whether this is in dealing with the recursive grief of the patient with dementia, the despair of the mother who has undergone an abortion or the anguish of those left behind by a sudden death. The justification is required because, as Bergman and Chalkley (2007:252) observe, there is an external presumption that the worker must have chosen the work 'so that the work that people do appears to provide insight into who they are' (Bergman & Chalkley, 2007:252). If dirty work is a choice that involves willing engagement with that which is physically, socially, morally or emotionally transgressive, then surely it stands to reason that those who chose such work are also transgressive, dirty, polluted and polluting. Just as those who are unable to maintain bodily control over defecation are taught to feel shame such that they may be judged unfit for society (Jervis, 2001), so those who willingly engage in with dirt must be stigmatised by their labours.

Whether they engage in dirty work under duress or by choice, dirty workers are well aware of the stigma attached to their occupations. Practically, the consequences for workers of such occupational stigma manifest in a sense of not being able to talk about such dirt with those outside their organisation or occupational group. Accordingly, nurses involved with genetic termination talk about 'unease and ambivalence on the part of the public' (Chiappetta-Swanson, 2005:105–6), and Samaritans dealing with callers who are emotionally distressed or suicidal comment on the way in which outsiders fear they may be 'tainted' if they 'get too close to suicide, upset or mental health issues' (Cath, Samaritan). The presence of these labourers as our agents of emotional dirty work is problematic – even polluting – because they reminds us of the fragile barrier that separates clean us from dirty other (Douglas, 1966; Miller, 1997 cited in Kreiner *et al.*, 2006). This point is reinforced in broader terms by Steve:

> When we joined, one of the first things they say when you join up is you'll lose some friends because they don't like you being a police officer. . . . Erm, I don't ordinarily tell people, I don't tell people I'm a police officer very often, because people change.
>
> (Steve, police officer)

It is our contention that among the range of factors that may taint an occupation is the emotional dirty work that workers are called upon to do, such that 'an individual who might have been received easily into ordinary social intercourse possesses a trait that can obtrude itself upon attention and turn those of us whom he [sic] meets away from him. . . . He possesses a stigma, an undesired differentness' (Goffman, 1997:73). Depression, suicide, and the grief associated with loss have the potential to be stigmatised and stigmatising. The burden, marginality and threat to order that they represent evoke the challenge 'how can you do it' (Ashforth & Kreiner, 1999). Even where such work is deemed necessary for the effective functioning of society, there is a generalised presumption that dirty work is deleterious work (Bergman & Chalkley, 2007; Haber *et al.*, 2011) undertaken by those with few alternatives (Hughes, 1958; Jervis, 2001). Given that external assessments of the worth of such work are so negative, how do those engaged in emotionally dirty tasks make sense of their labour? What if any positive sense of occupational identity can dirty workers construct?

Reframing, recalibrating and refocusing emotional dirty work

All forms of dirty work are, by definition, difficult, tainted and polluting. They speak to tasks that most of us would rather not know about or do. It is the work that is passed on to third parties who are often (though not always) employed at the lower levels of our organisational and occupational hierarchies. It is work at and across the boundaries of social acceptability. Consequently, there has been a long-held assumption that the experience of dirty work must be negative and that workers suffer low self-esteem and identity destruction (Kreiner *et al.*, 2006).

That individuals avoid dirty work tasks or leave occupations characterised by high levels of dirty work attests to the negative effects of such labour. There can be little doubt that many of us find different forms of dirty work disgusting or degrading (Simpson *et al.*, 2012). And yet, research evidence suggests that those who are employed in such tasks exhibit a much broader and more positive range of cognitive, behavioural and affective responses to dirty work and taint than is often presumed to be the case. Specifically, Ashforth and Kreiner (1999) note that workers make sense of the taint that arises from physical, social and moral dirt through three related processes: reframing, recalibrating and refocusing. Through these processes workers have been shown to construct positive occupational identities in the shadow of physically, socially and morally tainted work (Tracy & Scott, 2006). What has not been explored is whether or how reframing, recalibrating and refocusing might relate to sense making and identity construction when applied to emotionally tainted work. We address each of these points in turn in this section.

Within Ashforth and Kreiner's (1999:421) model, *reframing* refers to the techniques employed by workers to transform the 'meaning attached to a stigmatised occupation'. This tends to involve wrapping the dirty particulars of a job in more uplifting values, possibly stressing the broader mission and values of an occupation. For example, phone sex workers stress that their work is merely a service transaction like any other and one in which they perform a kind of social work, rather than focusing on caller masturbation and sin (Selmi, 2012); 'funeral directors state that they are helping relatives with grief, rather than processing dead bodies and profiting from their work (Thompson, 1991)' (Ashforth & Kreiner (1999:421). It is interesting to note that in the second example grief is seen as a consequence of other forms of dirt (rather than a form of dirt itself). By contrast, Sanders (2010) observed that veterinary technicians reluctantly engaged in a form of emotional dirty work every time they were required to comfort pet owners following the death of their animal. The physically and emotionally dirty work of veterinary technicians (with blood, body parts, euthanasia, disposal and the comforting of grieving owners) is framed in terms of an overriding love for animals and a relational concern for their owners. In this way work is made meaningful, even pleasurable (Sanders, 2010).

In terms of reframing emotional dirty work, our original research with Samaritans, an organisation providing listening support to people in emotional distress or with suicidal thoughts throughout the UK, revealed that, when talking to outsiders, Samaritans would downplay talk of suicide and distress in favour of emphasising their commitment to providing non-judgemental listening spaces and being there for people in need:

> It's having the feeling that you have helped someone that makes it worth while. Perhaps just that you have been there to listen to a concern that the caller has and feels isolated. Listening means that they don't think they are the only one.
>
> (Jo, Samaritan)

Where the dirty particulars of a job cannot be reframed by wrapping them in more uplifting values, occupational members may seek to *neutralise* their responsibility for the effects of a dirty task as part of the process of reframing. This is achieved through reference to the structural inevitability of act and outcome (Ashforth & Kreiner, 1999). For example, Samaritans are committed to taking calls from anyone in emotional need, even where, as in the case of paedophiles, they strongly disagree with the emotions and associated acts that are discussed during contact. Samaritans make sense of such work by referring back to their organisational commitment not to presume to know, judge or intervene in the lives of others. Interactions with the taboo emotions of such client groups are thus explained in terms of abiding by organisational rules (structures) and doing one's job. Moreover, responsibility for the thoughts and acts of the client are neutralised through reference to the anonymous nature of the 'call system' (Samaritans do not know who is calling, from where, or on which number) and the higher organisational values of being outwardly nonjudgemental and noninterventionist – all structural facets that remove responsibility for dirt and its effects from the labourer. If this process of neutralising does not succeed or clashes with a Samaritan's personal moral code or sense of responsibility, the person may eventually leave the organisation.

Another approach to making sense of the taints associated with dirty work is *recalibrating*. Recalibrating describes an attempt to adjust perceptions of the scope and depth of contact with dirt. Here the aim is to make the dirty aspect seem a smaller or less important part of the worker's role, part of a more favourable shared narrative on what it is that occupational members do (Ashforth & Kreiner, 1999). For example, airline cabin crew experience dirty work thanks to requirement for servility to others (not to mention the sexualisation of their image and role as part of the supposed glamour of flying (Hochschild, 1989)) and the need to placate disgruntled customers, calm the fearful and negotiate unwanted and inappropriate intimacy. However, when interviewed, cabin crew often seek to down play the significance of the sales and smiles components of their work, preferring instead to emphasise their core safety role. They work to recalibrate the place of dirt such that their knowledge of airline safety systems and associated skills in a crisis are brought to the fore. The requirement for emotional dirty work – dealing with passenger hysteria, anger or lust – is then repositioned as an issue of safety through the maintenance of control and order in times of crisis.

The third component of Ashforth and Kreiner's (1999:423) model is *refocusing*: '[W]hereas reframing actively transforms the stigmatised properties of dirty work and recalibration magnifies the redeeming qualities, refocusing actively overlooks the stigmatised properties. Occupational members wilfully dis-attend to the features of the work that are socially problematic.' We see this in Steve's account of inner-city police work – a context which is generally perceived to be difficult, dirty and dangerous (see Van Maanen 1978) – as he seeks to renarrate what it means to work with such communities so that they and he are seen in more positive terms:

> My history as a police officer has been in inner city estates. I've done that for five, six years and some go 'I couldn't do that' but I loved it. Because it's so . . . It becomes a class thing almost; but salt of the earth people and I like that because they tell you how it is. And I had a really good time there. And not that they were all victims; but they have a certain level of how they live and they're happy at that sort of level.
>
> (Steve, police officer)

Here, Steve's response to the dirty work of inner-city policing is loving it and having 'a good time'. He describes the communities with which he interacts as being composed of 'salt of the earth people', an expression used to denote persons of great worthiness, reliability and honesty. Here there is no reference to the aggression, abuse, violence, poverty or despair that he also experiences in the course of his work with the community. In a similar vein, exotic dancers refocus attention on the freedom, art and athleticism of their work as they seek to present dancing as a legitimate occupation (Grandy, 2008) while downplaying the lust that speaks to emotional and moral taint. Similarly, the attempts of pole dancers to refocus their occupation has culminated in the establishment of the World Pole Sport Fitness Championships (note how the use of 'fitness' speaks to notions of athleticism and virtue with no mention of dancing or emotion). Or we might consider veterinary technicians once more and their observed tendency to stress the technical and medical nature of their occupation when seeking to avoid discussion of the physical and emotional dirt (Sanders, 2010).

Thus it can be seen that processes of reframing, recalibrating and refocusing are employed by workers seeking to minimise and make sense of emotion-based taint. To these we would add a forth mode: *recasting*. Recasting describes an attempt to renarrate encounters with service recipients so as to make sense of or explain away transgressive or difficult emotional encounters. For example, when doctors' receptionists are on the receiving end of aggression, anger or verbal abuse from patients, they often recast the encounter as the emotional outpourings of someone who is ill or worried. The emotional dirt that must be handled by the receptionist is not taken as a personal attack but is instead recast as an unwanted effect of health concerns and, as such, is downplayed by the labourer. Members of the occupation then validate such downplaying where patients apologise for their transgression at a later date.

Our conversations with a veterinarian revealed a similar process of recasting when dealing with owners who decide to have their pet euthanised. In this case Ethan notes that the job of a vet is to look after people as well as animals, a task that includes making sense of the former's anger:

> it's not just treating the animal, it's treating the person and their emotions, and unfortunately if you don't understand that then I think you're in the wrong profession because to clients those animals are their babies, they're not a dog with a price tag on it. . . . (sighs) With aggression – I'm certainly not an aggressive person so I never take it quite personally, you just stay calm, you chat to them and you generally talk them round. But some of them are blaming you for the decision that they've made. On the one hand you've got to realise that actually the only reason they're being aggressive is because they're emotionally attached and they're not in control of those emotions, and so it's just letting them voice their opinions, get their emotion out, and then talking to them. . . . Erm so really when it comes to the dark side of euthanasia, the reason that we're euthanasing the animal is because it's starting to suffer. . . . I'm doing it for the animal and at the end of the day I'm stopping the animal suffering.
>
> (Ethan, veterinarian)

Ethan's account of the emotional dirty work required in veterinary practice, 'letting them voice their opinions' and getting 'their emotion out', chimes with Sanders's (2010) excellent research on veterinary technicians and dirty work in the United States. Both speak to occupational tasks that are emotionally troubling, demanding and unwanted. In addition to the blood, smells and bodies of animals, those in veterinary practice are subjected to the emotional trauma experienced by pet owners. In addition to grief and deep sorrow, workers such as Ethan must make sense of unwanted aggression. While rarely acceptable within the workplace, the dirty work of dealing with client aggression is recast as understandable insofar as owners thought of pets as 'their babies', with their aggression being a result of 'emotional attachment' and loss of 'control'. In the last line of Ethan's account we can also read recourse to *reframing through neutralisation* insofar as euthanasia is perceived as necessary, inevitable and moral.

To reiterate, those engaged in emotionally dirty work can be seen to make sense of the taint that arises from their labour through the same processes of reframing, refocusing and recalibrating that are observed in respect of physical, social and emotional dirt. We also introduce a fourth sense-making approach in respect of recasting. Through such methods, dirty workers strive to construct and maintain positive occupational identities and narratives. This tends to involve an attempt to maintain a separation between the worker, as agent of dirty work, and dirt itself, so as to minimise the taint associated with occupational tasks. It is, however, important to note that dirty workers do not always seek to distance themselves from dirt. Indeed, the ability to literately or symbolically stomach the dirt that others can not has often been observed to provide a particular type of occupational pride. In the materially and socially dirty work of garbage collectors and meat cutters, pride is express in physical strength (Meara, 1974). Meat cutters and nurses are known to revel in their fortitude when it comes to bodily fluids and death (McMurray, 2012; Meara, 1974). Those who work in butchery, nursing and home care are also proud of the training and technical skill they exhibit in dealing with different forms of dirt (McMurray, 2012). We find something similar in emotional dirty work. Samaritans talk of their work with people in emotional distress as a privilege and express satisfaction at having learnt to employ their empathetic listening skills (McMurray & Ward, 2014; Simpson *et al.*, 2011). Similarly, GP receptionists are rightly proud of their ability to perform emotional neutrality in the face of patient abuse (see Chapter 3), while making sense of such labour by recasting aggression as reflecting the fears of patients and relatives alike. In short, while emotional dirty work is often difficult, disruptive and unwanted work, this does not preclude it from being experienced as positive and satisfying work.

Conclusions

In this chapter we have consider the manner in which emotional labour might be contextualised as emotional dirty work. We have defined emotional dirty work as that which involves handling *'expressed feelings that threaten the solidarity, self-conception or preferred orders of a given individual or community . . . a subjective state assigned by either the individual involved or outside observers through which emotions are deemed to be in some sense polluting'* (McMurray & Ward, 2014:12 [original emphasis]). In essence this implies a need to work with emotions that are deemed out of place, contextually inappropriate, burdensome or taboo. While emotional dirty work may coincide with other forms of dirt, it demands attention (and study) as a phenomenon in and of itself. It may present as the core of an occupation's work, as in the case of Samaritans, or emerge as a component of working, managing and organising, as in the work of police officers, home carers, veterinarians, cabin crew, nurses and receptionists. This type of emotional labour is dirty because it is disruptive, often avoided by others, and passed on to third-party agents whose role it is to guard the boundary between organisational order and chaos and between the presumed good of calculative rationality on the one hand and apparent risks of unbridled emotion on the other.

Emotional dirty work is to be considered matter out of place because it often goes unseen, underacknowledged and underrewarded. Gendered as women's work, the emotional performances that are offered in response to such dirt are assumed to come naturally and easily to those who deploy such abilities. Because such work is positioned as an innate ability rather than a mastered skill, its claims for recognition go largely unheeded. Often passed down to those on the lower rungs of organisations, emotional dirty work is also tainted work insofar as it speaks to disorder, pollution and threat to good order. In these ways – as disorder, taint, pollutant and unrecognised imposition – emotional dirty work speaks of a dark side of emotional labour.

How do workers make sense of such dirt? Douglas (1966:38) suggests that there are several ways of treating such anomalies: 'Negatively, we can ignore, just not perceive them, or perceiving we can condemn. Positively we can deliberately confront the anomaly and try to create a new pattern of reality in which it has a place.' Through the practices of reframing, recalibrating and refocusing, dirty workers engage in both positive and negative forms of sense making. Dirty and tainted emotions may be ignored, downplayed, neutralised, marginalised, or justified as part of more uplifting messages and missions. To these processes we add the tendency to recast emotional dirt wherein workers attempt to renarrate confrontations with service recipients so as to make sense of or explain away transgressive or difficult emotional encounters. Finally, knowing that outsiders may condemn or fail to understand contact with emotional dirt, workers can find a sense of pride in being able to manage emotions that others can not stomach, as well as experiencing satisfaction at deploying what they see as skilled performances of emotional neutrality or empathy in response to the presentation of emotional dirt. Emotional dirty work can, then, be rewarding work. However, as considered in the next chapter, when such work is left unacknowledged and rewarded there is a danger that it will become toxic.

Note

1 The banking interviews with Sam and Ash were undertaken as part of a project on the banking crisis by Philip Linsley (York Management School, UK) and Robert McMurray. We thank Philip for agreeing to their use in this book.

5 Emotional pain and the threat of toxicity

So far, we have explored the ways in which organisations take advantage of workers' abilities to mask their genuine feelings to maintain a professional demeanour (see Chapter 3), to amplify their feelings of anger and frustration to intimidate others (see Chapter 2) and to engage in work that others would rather not acknowledge for fear of taint and contamination (see Chapter 4). So far our depiction of this dark side of emotional labour has been relatively optimistic. Our aim has been to argue that not all emotional labour must by definition be a negative or dissonance-inducing experience. As we have shown in respect of home carers and Samaritans, dealing with difficult emotions can be a source of pride, while the negative connotations associated with such labour can be refocused, reframed, recalibrated or recast such that they are downplayed (see Chapter 4). In short, working with the dark side of emotional labour can be a positive experience.

While we have sought to problematise simplistic dichotomies that hold emotional labour as necessarily harmful, we recognise that such work is often difficult work with negative consequences. Accordingly, in this chapter we explore instances, experiences and firsthand accounts of those who have struggled to cope with the pain and toxicity of organisational life. Organisational life can be painful because customers can be unreasonable, because some coworkers are manipulative, because bosses ask for the impossible, because our efforts can go unrewarded, because the experience of work can be disempowering and, as we have seen throughout this book, because dealing with the emotions of self and other can be exceedingly, even unremittingly, demanding. Here we outline an argument that positions emotional pain as an inevitable by-product of organisational life. By drawing on our own interviews with cabin crew, an HR director and a lawyer, as well as illustrative stories of emotional distress covered in the media, we support Frost (2003) in demonstrating that such organisational pain has the potential to turn into something more sinister and arguably more dangerous: emotional toxicity. We note also that the danger of toxicity is often averted by those unsung emotion workers whom Frost (2003) identifies as 'toxin handlers'.

It is on those who handle the emotional pain of organisational life that we focus our attention in this chapter. With accounts from Rachel, an HR director; Claire, a member of a cabin crew; Hannah, a primary school teacher; and Teresa, a bouncer, we consider the extent to which these so-called toxin handlers informally and formally engage in complex forms of emotion management to help relieve the suffering of their colleagues. Drawing on the sparse extant literature on emotional toxicity, we question the extent to which organisations benefit and profit from these informal mechanisms of coping that are effectively 'gifted' (Bolton, 2000) by key individuals who appear to have a capacity to manage the complex, difficult and messy emotions of others.

To explore these issues, we begin with a discussion of organisational pain. In this section we specifically explore a variety of sources from which pain can derive. We offer examples from our own empirical research that support some of Frost's '7 Deadly Ins' and others that suggest there might be other sources of emotional pain that are inherent in work itself. Following this, we then seek to illustrate examples in which emotional pain has transformed into emotional toxicity. We conclude with firsthand accounts of some of the methods of coping with repeated exposure to emotional pain and some of the potential consequences for those who take on the role of toxin handler.

Emotional pain

It is safe to say that we have all, in one way or another, experienced emotional pain, stress or discomfort at the hands of an organisation. Reapplying for a job you have done for more than 15 years as a consequence of a strategic redundancy round, managing the morale of your team in light of unrealistic expectations and targets from above, or working alongside someone whom you cannot trust – these are just some of the situations that can and do cause emotional pain in any organisation. For Frost, such 'pain is a fact of organisational life' (2003:12) arising out of what he calls the 'deadly Ins'.

'Deadly Ins'

In his captivating book *Toxic Emotions at Work*, Frost identifies seven 'deadly Ins' (2003:36), seven potential sources of emotional pain within organisations. These are *In*tention (where managers purposefully degrade others); *In*competence (from managers who lack the ability to craft meaningful relationships with their subordinates); *In*fidelity (an erosion of trust or sense of betrayal); *In*sensitivity (a lack of empathy, compassion and political appreciation); *In*trusion (work-life balance issues); *In*stitutional Forces (policies that hurt workers and erode their confidence); and *In*evitability (unintended consequences of change, sudden death of a coworker). By ways of illustration we describe the experience and effects of these 'Ins' across two very different work settings: that of the teacher and that of the Human Resources director.

Hannah, a primary school teacher with eight years' experience, speaks of the way in which the *In*stitutional forces of the English education system have eroded her aspirations and enthusiasm for teaching. In this example, Hannah describes the wearing effects of unwanted bureaucracy:

> I think over the years I've felt it more . . . it's actually quite tiring . . . over the years the constraints of the curriculum, inspections, the negative aspects of my job have overtaken . . . driven by targets and achievement and content that I find quite exhausting . . . it's the pressure of not having time for them [children] in the way that I want to.
>
> (Hannah, primary school teacher)

Where Hannah once felt excitement, passion and a strong commitment to the social, moral and educational development of the children in her charge, she now feels exhaustion and pressure from the wider school system. Targets, constraints and time pressures mean that she increasingly characterises her occupational experiences negatively. This negative emotional response can be seen to 'flow from everyday . . . practices that hurt the people that carry them out' (Frost, 2003:45). Of course, it is not the intention of the education system to erode the enthusiasm and passion of its teaching professionals. Rather, this result is an unwanted and unforeseen by-product of the systems and processes that were initially designed to support and propagate best practice. Nonetheless, the bureaucracy and associated institutional forces emerge as a source of emotional pain.

Our next illustration arguably concerns *Intention, Infidelity, Incompetence* and *Insensitivity*. It is based on HR director Rachel's account of a critical incident with her managing director and a salesperson. Here we can read the intersection of four of Frost's 'deadly Ins':

> *Rachel*: There was a guy who worked in our men's wear department who was a bit quiet but he was very very effective. He was quite young but he was a very good sales person. . . . But our Managing Director made him really nervous. . . . Every time the Managing Director came by he [the young guy] would end up saying something really stupid or looking a bit clumsy because he was nervous.
>
> The Managing Director would say: 'What are you doing about him? He is crap. Get rid of him.'
>
> I [Rachel] would reply: 'He is not; he is actually quite a good salesman and runs a really good back stock. It's you that makes him nervous . . . he just feels a bit intimidated by you, just give him a chance.'
>
> *And I [Rachel] kept sticking up for this lad. But then there was an incident of shop lifters [thieves] on the floor and it was when this lad was on duty and it wasn't anything to do with this lad, as in, it wasn't his fault.*
>
> But the Managing Director said: 'Well it was because he was on duty. That's it, I told you he was rubbish. Get rid of him. . . . He is crap. I want you to sack him.'

I told him: 'We can't, he has worked for us for over two years he has got full employment rights. So even if I did, it's not legal. And besides which it's not right anyway because on what grounds? I can't just say the Managing Director doesn't like your face and thinks you're [*sic*] rubbish.'

Managing Director: 'I don't care, I am telling you to do it, I am the Managing Director you are one of my directors you do that tomorrow.'

So I had to go in the next day, get this poor young lad in and say I am really sorry. . . . Three weeks later we got the form for industrial tribunal for unfair dismissal. But the Managing Director still said it was my fault because if I had got rid of him in the first place when I had been first told to it would never have happened. So emotionally I didn't handle that very well at all. That was awful. It was horrendous.

(Rachel, HR director)

From Rachel's perspective, the MD's judgements of the salesperson and his treatment of her as a colleague demonstrate *In*competence in that he was unable to form a meaningful relationship with either of them and continued to pursue a line of action based on his personal feelings without taking into consideration the political, legal and financial implications, thus giving the lie to the idea of neutral management and rational organising. The labelling of staff as 'crap' speaks to *In*tention insofar as he deliberately degraded others. Then there is *In*fidelity; rather than respecting Rachel's feedback or indeed her pleas for reconsideration, the MD inflicted emotional pain on both her and the salesperson. In conversation Rachel explained that this emotional pain was a direct result of the MD's *in*sensitivity in terms of a lack of empathy, compassion and political appreciation. In this way, several of Frost's (2003) *In*s combine to make a painful working situation.

Interestingly, Frost's (2003) identification of these potential sources of emotional pain focus almost entirely on methods of organising, managing and policing an organisation with a particular focus on management's and leadership's abilities to inflict pain on those that they manage. This assumption continues to underpin the subsequent work described in the limited extant literature that has followed Frost, including Gallos (2008) and Stein (2007). Whilst we do not dispute that these sources of pain and toxicity are prevalent in organisations today, we also have accounts that suggest there may be other sources of pain and potential toxicity in the nature and context of the work itself. As we consider, these other sources of pain have varying levels of visibility.

Task-related pain

Claire has worked for a full-service national airline carrier as cabin crew for more than 20 years. Her work is both physically and emotionally challenging and, as is evident in her comments, sometimes emotionally painful:

> You are surrounded by people all of the time. After service you want time when people aren't looking at you. Every 20 minutes we have to walk the cabin and check the toilets. We have to constantly watch and monitor passengers, we are looking for people who are drinking too much . . . the hidden problem of drugs, older people get[ting] confused . . . I love it when I get into my hotel room and shut the door and no one can see me!
>
> (Claire, cabin crew)

The inherent visibility of Claire's role as cabin crew is something she experiences as painful, causing her to withdraw from the world to recharge and perhaps heal in order for her to continue working as cabin crew with all that it entails. She is essentially both the source and the subject of surveillance in that it is her job to watch and monitor passengers whilst they simultaneously observe her doing so. For Claire, being unable to escape the 'front stage' (Goffman, 1959), particularly within the confines of an aircraft, is, she feels, taking an emotional toll on her well-being.

Similarly, Teresa's work as a door attendant is painful and pervasive but for very different reasons. Despite being a five-foot three-inch mother of two, Teresa has 'worked the doors', alongside men twice her stature, for almost ten years. During this time she has been stabbed, has witnessed a suicide and has been physically assaulted seven times and verbally abused on a regular basis. She speaks of the effects that this part of the work has had on her over time and how she is particularly sensitive to threats of personal attack:

> Friends of mine have been jumped on the way home . . . you get told to look out for challenges and repercussions especially when you have to chuck somebody out of a place and they've kicked and screamed all the way out the door . . . they usually shout abuse back at you . . . 'I'll get you! Mind your back! I'll stab you when you're passing!' . . . I'm very wary when I get home and I'm sort of . . . on guard . . . every time something happens I'm at the windows or I'm at the doors, it takes me a couple of days to sort of . . . calm down and get over it, but it does make me very uneasy.
>
> (Teresa, bouncer)

Door-work is undeniably dangerous work in a 'threat to life' sense, but, as Teresa points out, it is also emotionally difficult work in that she has been witness to situations of extreme violence whilst simultaneously being charged with the responsibility of protecting those involved. Here visibility refers both to that which is experienced and witnessed ('shout abuse back at you') to the fear of the unseen (at home 'I'm at the windows or I'm at the doors') as Teresa struggles with the emotional pressure of having to 'mind your back' as a consequence of work tasks and their aftermath. She tells of the ongoing effects of this work and how she herself has to live with it on a day-to-day basis:

> it's the serious fights that you try to block out because they can . . . they can affect you . . . you know if you're sitting at home quiet and, then, all of a sudden you can start shaking because all of the emotions come back up from . . . the anger and everything else.
>
> (Teresa, bouncer)

The observable dark side of Teresa's work resides in the everyday violence and abuse that she witnesses at the door. It is work that requires the deployment of both antipathetic emotional labour and emotional neutrality as part of an embodied encounter with other. But it is also dark because of the emotional impacts that are less readily seen: in the sudden 'shaking' and emotions that 'come back up from . . . the anger' long after the event itself is over. This is the 'sticky mark or residue' (to borrow from Bergman & Chalkley, 2007) that speaks to the lingering existence of pain that, if unobserved and unchecked, can fester into something much more severe and arguably more dramatic: emotional toxicity.

Emotional toxicity

For Frost (2003:5), emotional toxicity suggests 'elements that can poison, whether a person or an entire system; toxins spread and seep, often undetected, in various degrees'. Frost (2003) clearly has an agenda to change the ways in which organisations and individuals address sources of emotional pain so as to prevent them turning toxic. We concur but would add that it is also necessary to consider that pain which arises from the *content* of occupational tasks themselves and not just the *Ins* that arise from methods of organising, managing and policing an organisation. Fixing organisational structures and relations will go only so far if the source of the pain is the job itself. If the pain inherent in work tasks is left unrecognised, it can become toxic. If the resulting toxicity is not recognised then it can, in turn, erupt unexpectedly.

Use of the term 'toxicity' to describe organisational phenomena is both strong and evocative. The ability of the metaphor to evoke images or ideas of dramatic, catastrophic events such as large-scale redundancy programs or the death of a coworker is undoubtedly part of the concept's appeal. And yet, Gallos (2008:356) argues that 'the power of the concept is in its pervasiveness'. What she means by this is that just as toxic contamination can be an overt, dramatic or visible process (as in the case of door staff and violence), there are other contexts in which it is slow, pervasive and invisible (as in the bureaucratic erosion of a teacher's enthusiasm). In the latter sense, ongoing sources of emotional pain associated with an organisation or task slowly degrade capacity, potentially spreading infection or malaise to those who come into contact with it. Where such emotional pain is invisible or forced underground, there is a danger that it may lie silently poised to erupt unexpectedly (Gallos, 2008). What follows are first- and secondhand accounts of incidents that can be conceptualised as an unexpected eruption of emotional toxicity, where the emotional pain endured by workers has finally come to a head and is now toxic, corrosive and, in some cases, contagious.

For Rachel, an HR director, the situation with her managing director continued to decline until she finally snapped:

> it just deteriorated . . . and degenerated into me saying you are a prat [laughs] completely giving into my emotions.
>
> (Rachel, HR director)

This dramatic outburst of feelings also included her slamming the boardroom door for added dramatic effect. Finally, Rachel resigned from her post as HR director in favour of a sideways move. Rachel explained that this explosion of emotion arose out of a long-term deterioration in her relationship with the MD. She described ongoing examples of *in*competence, *in*fidelity and *in*sensitivity that were exacerbated by a breakdown in communication such that the head of the organisation would leave her notes rather than communicate with her directly. Rachel recalls how these notes 'became known as the poison pen letters that would appear on the desk saying "well what are you doing about this" and I would say "well I've already handled it" . . . it was like a marriage where you think "I just need to get a divorce now".' A failure in communication led everyday pain to become toxic, with that underground toxicity eventually exploding in confrontation and resignation.

Where Rachel speaks to the pain and toxicity or organised relations, Claire speaks to the manner in which the very work of cabin crew has led both her and her colleagues to experience emotional pain. Again, unattended, such pain threatens to transmute into a potent form of toxicity:

> The job has got harder over the years. We have a lot less rest and suffer from exhaustion and depression. The suicide rate for cabin crew is very high compared to other jobs. It is very common to hear of crew having breakdowns. One woman stripped all her clothes off and jumped on the conveyor belt with a stuffed giraffe under her arm. Another locked herself in her hotel room for three days on a stopover and smeared excrement and urine all over the walls. We are on our own. When I go away I spend 99% of the time alone. I love to close that door and be on my own. . . . Sometimes at home, I shut myself in the back bedroom where

no one can see me. It overlooks nothing and I just sit in there because it is quiet and I am on my own.

(Claire, cabin crew)

What is evident in her account is the way in which she is resigned to the idea that part and parcel of the work is the ability to endure, manage and perhaps at some point fail to manage the pain associated with the pressure, performances and self-management required of cabin crew. When the pain cannot be managed it has become personally toxic as workers suffer suicide and breakdowns. Indeed, thanks to social media it is not difficult to find reports of cabin crew breakdowns and in some cases even video footage of the event. Some examples include a Jet Blue flight attendant who went on to the public address system, swore at a passenger whom he claimed treated him rudely, grabbed a beer and slid down onto the tarmac using the emergency chute before driving home (*The Guardian*, 2011). Then there is the American Airlines flight attendant who ranted and screamed that the plane was going to crash (*New York Daily News*, 2012) and the American Eagles flight attendant who, after a flight had been significantly delayed, allegedly announced over the public address system, 'If anyone has the balls to want to get off, I'll let you get off! Get off!' (*Huffington Post*, 2012). Here we have examples of personal pain turning toxic for the individual and organisation alike. To be clear, such toxicity is not a consequence of individual failings. The ability to cope or endure may be altered by variations in individual workers' emotional capital (see Chapter 6), but the pain described here arises from the very nature of the work. It becomes toxic in the absence of informal and formal organised mechanisms for acknowledging or alleviating such pain. Where untreated, the potential for eruption carries the risk of costs for the individual (ill health, breakdown, resignation, sacking) and for the organisation (bad publicity, poor services, legal ramifications).

In other contexts the threat of toxicity is not in dramatic and public breakdown but instead is more subtle and pervasive. Jane and John, two veteran Samaritan volunteers, speak of calls that have 'stayed with them' because of their particularly emotionally challenging nature.

I had one a couple of weeks ago and called an ambulance and felt I probably did not do them a service because their life was so terrible suicide may have been what they really wanted. So I feel difficult about that.

(Jane, Samaritan)

I still struggle with a call from someone killing themselves with anorexia that had two children. This has stayed with me knowing that it is going on now.

(John, Samaritan)

Although they took these calls some time ago, the pain associated with them continues to haunt both Jane and John. The 'difficult' feelings that have 'stayed with' these Samaritans suggest that in spite of their best efforts to work through the emotional pain that is an essential part of the role, it has not gone away. The pain lingers despite a range of formal and informal mechanisms that exist within the organisation for addressing the necessary pain of the work. Where the pain of work becomes too much, workers may chose to exit an organisation. Such organisational exit is often an indicator of and a method for coping with emotional pain that has become toxic. Samaritan work, providing empathetic listening spaces for callers in emotional distress, is often impeded by sex calls. Answering a call from a heavy breather, masturbator or fantasist is not uncommon for a Samaritan. From the organisation's and the volunteers' perspectives, these are unwanted calls that are felt to block the phone lines for those who may be in real need, while also wasting the time and emotional energy of Samaritans themselves. As Katie notes:

> Some nights I can go home feeling really grubby. When you have just had . . . say 6 sex calls and nothing else, it leaves you feeling dirty and frustrated. It's the content of the calls and the manipulation. It really gets to you. You get fed up when it is just these calls. You think 'How dare you? That's "not what I'm here for".'
>
> (Katie, Samaritan)

While Katie can vent these frustrations to coworkers and shift leaders, the pain caused by these unwanted calls stays with her, threatening to become toxic. For some, the inability to get past the pain of sex calls causes them to leave Samaritan. As Alex, a trainee Samaritan, reflects on his wife's past experience of being a Samaritan:

> my wife was a Samaritan . . . for about 3 or 4 years and then stopped because of the, all the sexual abuse. The sex calls . . . she just couldn't be bothered with that.

While some Samaritans dismissed sex calls as nothing much to worry about, other Samaritans struggled to cope with the thoughts, emotions and expressed deeds of sex calls or the unwanted images they 'clearly want to put in my head' (Joss, Samaritan). Where the pain of such encounters cannot be dealt with through organisational systems of debriefing and counselling, the threat of exit, in response to or in fear of situations that are personally toxic, was very real.

As employees of an organisation that specialises in supporting those in emotional distress, Samaritans are very much aware of the dangers of emotional toxicity, and not just from unwanted sex calls. One of our first meetings with the organisation brought forward discussions of the longer-term consequences of exposure to emotional pain, including an increase in emotional volatility, burnout and empathy fatigue. Such compassion fatigue (Figley, 1995), could be observed in other contexts, including that of the legal work of Alex a retired lawyer:

> There is a danger urm . . . urm . . . after 37 years of dealing with matrimonial problems you can become very cynical [laughs] you know? I have heard it all before . . . you would hear the same stories time and time again.
>
> (Andrew, retired lawyer)

These accounts raise the issue of whether too much exposure to too much emotional pain for too long can result in a slow and subtle erosion of feeling, sensitivity and empathy, something akin to Mestrovic's (1997) ideas of postemotionality, in which those who are exposed to heightened emotions become desensitised to them. Parallels of these concerns can be heard in a number of the accounts of work documented in Terkel's book *Working* (1974). One pertinent examples is that of Bob, an Emergency Rescue Squad member who is terrified by the possibility of losing his ability to connect with his own emotional experiences as a consequence of becoming hardened by his day-to-day work:

> I'm afraid that after seein' so much of this [pain and suffering] I can come home and hear my kid in pain and not feel for him. So far it hasn't happened. I hope to God it never happens. I hope to God I always feel. When my grandmother passed away a couple of months ago, I didn't feel anything. I wonder . . . is it happening to me?
>
> (Terkel, 1974:575)

And yet he clings on to the hope that his emotional responsiveness remains intact:

> This morning I read the paper about that cop that was shot. His six-year-old son wrote a letter: 'Hope you get better, Dad.' My wife was fixin' breakfast. I said, 'Did you read the paper, hon?' She says, 'Not yet.' 'Did you read the letter this cop's son sent to his father when he was in the hospital?' She says, 'No.' 'Well, he's dead now.' So I read the part of it and I started to choke. I says, 'What the hell . . .' I dropped the paper just to get my attention away. I divided my attention to my son that was in the swing. What the hell. All the shit I seen and did and I gotta read a letter . . . but it made me feel like I'm still maybe a while away from feeling like I have nothing left to feel. I still had feelings left. I still have quite a few jobs to go.
>
> (Terkel, 1974:578)

For Stein (2007:1234) 'a key feature of toxicity is that it cannot be absorbed or processed'. This rather abrupt and confronting possibility is what separates toxicity from pain. While pain is an inevitable part of organisational life that can be and often is addressed through the sharing of emotional difficulties, toxicity speaks to the long-term personal and systemic effects of failing to acknowledge and alleviate pain. Toxicity is a poison that spreads if left untreated. Toxicity threatens the well-being of individual workers and the functioning of entire systems, such that professionals succumb to passion fatigue, workers lock themselves in quiet rooms and those unfairly sacked threaten legal action.

Given Frost's (2003) assertion that pain is an inevitable consequence of organisational living, it is perhaps surprising that there is not more evidence of toxicity in firsthand and media accounts of working and managing. This may reflect underreporting, but it might also be thanks to the largely unseen emotion work of 'toxin handlers'.

Toxin handlers

As we have seen in the preceding sections of this chapter, emotional pain is an inevitable by-product of organisational life. For Frost (2003) this emotional pain is caused by one or more of the '7 deadly Ins', which are effectively organising practices. We have noted from our own research that emotional pain can also be a consequence of the inherent nature of the work itself. Without intervention, treatment or dispersion, such emotional pain has the potential to become much more sinister and dangerous as it becomes toxic. We have demonstrated that emotional toxicity can take on many forms affecting both the organisation and the individual, including and yet not limited to public and dramatic emotional breakdowns, quiet organisational exists, volatility and compassion fatigue (Figley, 1995).

Working with Frost's (2003) premise that emotional pain is an inevitable by-product of organisational life and Stein's (2007:1234) characterisation of emotional toxicity as that which is neither 'absorbed [n]or processed', we assert, along with others (including Gallos, 2008), that the work of toxin handlers is crucial in managing the relationship between emotional pain and emotional toxicity. The remainder of this chapter seeks to explore the emotion management practices of those whom we have identified as toxin handlers from our own data through the lens of both informal and formal toxin-handling approaches. We end our chapter with a discussion of the extent to which all toxin handling continues to be effectively 'gifted' (Bolton, 2000; Gallos, 2008) emotional labour as a consequence of organisations' continually undervaluing and underappreciating the role, nature and consequences of the emotion management required of toxin handlers who work to keep organisational pain from becoming toxic.

Informal toxin handling

The idea of being exposed to, witnessing or working with dark, difficult and challenging emotions is not a prospect that all of us relish. The same holds for dealing with the emotional pain of others, and yet individuals take it upon themselves to alleviate such pain and so reduce the chances of toxicity erupting within their organisations. Take, for example, Claire's account of her highly informal approach to her cabin crew's expressing their emotional pain:

> I have a giggle with them [crew] in the galley and muck around and things because it makes them more relaxed. It is fine with me if they come in and kick the bin or throw a grape or a peanut because you have to relieve your tension somewhere.
>
> (Claire, cabin crew)

Here then, the emotional pain, tension and frustration experienced by Claire's team of cabin crew are relieved in mischievous and constrained acts of resistance or organisational 'misbehaviour' (Ackroyd & Thompson, 1999). Allowing her crew to break a rule of conduct or act in a way unbecoming of cabin crew in a 'back-stage' area – away from the continuous observation and scrutiny of both passengers and the airlines – permits them an emotional release. In this example, Claire, as toxin handler, is not necessarily actively absorbing the emotional pain of others, but she is creating the emotional space that is conducive to their processing the negativity they might feel.

Thinking about toxin handling in this way allows us to consider other processes and methods that might be usefully employed to alleviate some of the emotional pain experienced within organisations. In her recent book Kathryn Waddington (2012) considers the relationship between emotion and gossip, in particular the extent to which acts of gossiping can alleviate emotional pain, specifically how 'gossiping might also have a protective function for employees and organizations, preventing the build up of feelings that it is inappropriate to express or display in public' (Waddington, 2012:71). By preventing the 'buildup' of inappropriate feelings, gossip can perhaps be seen as method of toxin handling. In fact, drawing on Obholzer's (2005) psychodynamic understandings of emotions as 'psychic raw material', Waddington (2012:71) goes so far as to state that 'gossiping . . . can be seen as a form of "organizational detox"'. Although the act of gossiping may alleviate tension, thereby protecting employees and the organisation, its cathartic qualities may be short lived as it fails to address the underlying and longer-term issues and problems that are the source of the emotional pain. Analysis of the issue is further complicated by Gallos's (2008:358) assertion that venting or dumping pain carries the risk of spreading and escalating emotional pain, perhaps even to the point to which it becomes toxic: 'toxic dumping contaminates a broad range of organisational processes and outcomes, impacts innocent bystanders, and weakens collective capacitates to break the escalating spiral'.

In this sense, the risk of contamination is not just to the 'toxin handler' who is called upon to use his or her emotion management skills to offer an ear or share a reassuring word but is much wider. Such a conceptualisation compels us to consider the extent to which all workers, at some point or another, act as informal toxin handlers to colleagues. To what extent is this a hidden and yet invaluable resource that organisations use on a day-to-day basis, allowing companies to create working environments and enact organisational processes that are imbued with pain and darkness with limited consequence? As informal toxin handlers, workers are effectively 'gifting' (Bolton, 2000b) their emotional work to support colleagues as they seek to find ways of preventing their emotional pain from becoming toxic.

Extending Waddington's (2012) and Gallos's (2008) discussions of gossip and venting, we position these acts or processes as informal methods of toxin handling. Despite the associated longer-term risks to the organisation and the short-term gains to those in emotional pain, many organisations and individuals rely heavily on these informal methods of processing the darker side of the work that they do. Doctors' receptionists vent to colleagues about difficult encounters with patients, restaurant wait staff talk to each other about rude customers and prison officers often talk through violent encounters with prisoners. An account from Dawn, a Samaritan, demonstrates the effectiveness of such informal toxin handling in which coworkers empathise and appreciate the pain that is being experienced. In this particular case the immediacy of the pain experienced by a fellow Samaritan volunteer was stifling and required a compassionate and timely response in order for their work to continue:

> And the other thing is, if the person you are on with gets distressed. I have had that recently actually, they just burst into tears [laughs]. I think they were on the call at the time, the caller couldn't hear they were upset, but it touched them somehow and off they went. Crying. So I took my phone off and when they had finished their call their phone came off and we just had a cup of tea and a talk. She cried all the time but she had to. Then we recovered and got back on.
>
> (Dawn, Samaritan)

In this case, the 'tea and talk' were enough to sufficiently alleviate the pain triggered by that particular call. As we observed and were told so often at Samaritans, despite the excellent formal debriefing (toxin-handling) systems that existed within the organisation, for many Samaritans there continued to be a preference for a more informal approach. These Samaritans expressed their preference for talking through difficult calls with other volunteers they felt close to or had a connection with rather than using the official channels.

Others saw value in both methods, particularly those new to the organisation and the pain that the work could involve. For an organisation committed to supporting the emotional well-being of its volunteers, this posed a number of challenges as it rendered at least some of the emotional support work, that is, the toxin handling, invisible to the wider organisation.

Formal toxin handling

Dawn's account of why she didn't make it as a counsellor implies just how essential a toxin handler's emotional labour skills are in facilitating the processing of difficult emotions and challenging situations:

> Back in the early '90s I was training to be a counsellor . . . I thoroughly enjoyed it . . . but I didn't feel the support structure . . . was very good. I had three small children and I could only counsel in the evenings and I had some really tricky cases very early on. And my tutor wasn't keen, by the time I got home at half past ten at night, she wasn't particularly keen for me to ring her up and go blaaaa down the phone, I felt. So it was stressing me. . . . I thought this is no fun, time to stop. So I didn't actually fully complete the training, I sort of dropped out just before the end.
> (Dawn, counsellor)

Despite 'thoroughly enjoying' the work of counselling, Dawn chose to leave this particular organisation because of a perceived lack of emotional support from her tutor. In this case the formal organisational system of debriefing to the tutor was ineffective as a consequence of what was perceived by Dawn as poor emotion management. Rather than feeling encouraged to discuss and explore difficult emotions and emotional pain in a timely manner, Dawn felt her emotional needs were framed as an unwanted burden, given that her tutor did not encourage her calling at a late hour. The result – as suggested earlier in other contexts of emotional pain where the individual is no longer able to cope – is that Dawn left the organisation. Whether Dawn's account of the support on offer was shared by others is beyond the scope of our discussion. However, the lack of support could be interpreted as a sign of the tutor's own compassion fatigue (Figley, 1995) resulting from a buildup of pain that had become toxic (Hatfield *et al.*, 1994). Alternatively, the tutor may have had a different appreciation of what counted as 'timely' toxin handling in a formal sense.

In a bid to illustrate the emotional complexity of the work undertaken by those formally appointed as toxin handlers, we can draw on Rachel's vibrant account of the emotionality that imbued her working life. As an HR director she had a formal concern for the welfare of employees. This concern went well beyond the immediate confines of work:

> I would have my agenda of what I wanted to do for the day, somebody would come into my office sit on the sofa and burst into tears. . . . There

were problems of people not getting on with each other and having to mediate with that. Or people with things going on at home, they had found out their husband had cancer and it was dealing with that as well, illness – a wider range of things. And you tend to deal with that so that the business doesn't suffer but you are looking after that person and providing a duty of care to them as well.

(Rachel, HR director)

Rachel's willingness to listen and support workers with such a wide range of emotional issues is clearly driven by her understanding of the potentially toxic nature of emotional pain. Not only that, she appears willing to deal with pain derived from both within the organisation and beyond, based on an appreciation that pain – whatever its source – has implications for the welfare of the individual and the success of the business ('you tend to deal with that so that the business doesn't suffer'). The concern for the individual is expressed in terms of a duty: 'looking after that person and providing a duty of care to them as well'. And yet, being exposed to such a variety and intensity of third-party emotional pain and then having to cope with the lived reality of working practices that surround such work was not undertaken without effect. At one level, the time taken handling the emotional pain of others resulted in Rachel having to working late to complete the tasks she had set out to do and make difficult decisions about whether and how to report emotional concerns up and down the hierarchy insofar as they represented an HR issue, while also taking on the additional work involved in resolve disputes between others and operating within the constraints of organisational rules and procedures. To these were added personal physical effects:

I would soak it in all day and be neutral and very empathetic and do all those things, and . . . I am a bit of a sponge for it and I get a lot of tension in my neck and shoulders and I used to be really bad with that . . . because it has got to affect you somehow.

(Rachel, HR director)

With the help of a sponge metaphor Rachel describes how she felt she was absorbing the emotional pain of the employees, to somehow relieve them of a burden that had the potential to turn toxic. This is akin to Borysenko's (1988) use of the 'psychic sponge' metaphor to describe those who had a tendency, often unconscious, to absorb the emotions of those around them. These ideas became the foundation of the emotional contagion construct (see Pugh, 2001; Barsade, 2002; Hatfield *et al.*, 2004; Barger & Grandey, 2006). And yet, the dark, difficult, sad and challenging emotions she absorbed did not just disappear. Instead she had effectively become the organisation's septic tank in which challenging and difficult emotions were deposited. Rachel saw a direct link between the physical pain she experienced in her neck and shoulders and the emotional pain she absorbed at work. The relationship between physical and emotional pain is one explored at some length by Frost (2003) and continues to permeate the extant literature on emotional toxicity (Frost & Robinson, 1999; Rein, McCraty & Atkinson, 1995).

When Rachel decided to leave her role, news of her move spread quickly, and worker reactions were perhaps testament to the effectiveness of Rachel's emotional labouring abilities as a toxin handler:

> when I said I was not going to do the personnel any more, I had a stream of staff coming to me and saying you can't not be the person because *who will we go to with our problems, and who will sort everything out for us and who will make it all ok?*
>
> (Rachel, HR director, emphasis added)

It is from this quote that we derived the title of this chapter; we chose it for two main reasons. First, for us at least, it emphasises the width and breadth of toxin handlers' work, much of which is often invisible and under-valued by the wider organisation. Second, it gives a flavour of the emotional intensity and responsibility of the role and its importance to those who draw upon it to survive and navigate the emotional pain they experience as a lived reality of their daily lives. To talk of pain as an inevitable consequence of organising is to invite discussion of the different forms that the dark side of work can take, from Frost's (2003) '7 deadly Ins' through the pain of everyday work tasks and on to toxicity that can fester or erupt. The point of naming such pain is to make it visible. In making it visible, we can begin to consider the ways in which such pain might be handled and, in so doing, begin to appreciate the value of those charged with formal and informal processes of toxin handling.

Conclusion

The idea that organisations can create emotional pain for employees, customers and various other stakeholders is by no means a revelation. Organisation theory has developed a substantive appreciation for the role and presence of pain in a wide range of organisational phenomena, including resistance (Alvesson & Willmott, 2002), harassment (Collinson & Collinson, 1996), humour (Schnurr & Chan, 2011; Sanders, 2004) and cynicism (Carey, 2014). The focus of this chapter has been on the role that particular individuals within all organisations play in mitigating, preventing and helping to process the emotional pain that occurs as a natural by-product of organisational life. The emotional work they undertake is sometimes part of their employment contract, particularly in the case of middle managers, but more often than not it is emotional labour that is 'gifted' to the organisation by well-meaning and, often, emotionally resilient individuals.

The emotional work undertaken, either formally or informally, by toxin handlers is often difficult, challenging and uncomfortable work in that they are exposed to a variety of emotional states and are privy to highly personal and often sensitive details and also in that they have no formal training or support for processing and coping with what they hear. Once, again, these everyday emotional heroes are labouring on the dark side as they work to prevent emotional pain degrading into something entirely more noxious – emotional toxicity.

As we have demonstrated in this chapter, the metaphor of emotional toxicity is compelling and attention grabbing. For Stein (2007:1236) the image evoked by the term 'toxicity' 'encapsulates the notion of experiences that are felt to be poisonous and that cannot easily be dealt with'. Toxicity spreads through the organisation, polluting and contaminating those who are unfortunate enough to get too close. Extending this characterisation, Gabriel's 'miasma' might usefully be noted here, not as another metaphor for describing organisational states but as 'a concept that describes the contagious state of pollution, material, psychological, moral and spiritual, that afflicts all who work in particular organisations' (Gabriel, 2012:1139). Importantly, however, our own research has challenged the concept of emotional toxicity in two key ways. First, we draw attention to more subtle, reserved and yet nonetheless emotionally distressing manifestations of toxicity. Toxicity can build up to the point that it can be contained no longer and finally erupts. When these toxic eruptions take place, they can be dramatic and public outbursts that can be shocking enough to make headline news. And yet we argue that emotional toxicity can also present as thoughts and feelings that stain, haunt or linger in that they taint or colour the experiences and emotional well-being of the individual. These experiences of toxicity can manifest as emotional volatility and/or compassion fatigue.

Whether the buildup of emotional pain and toxicity is one that is dramatic and public or silent and private, it is evident that there will be consequences for the wider organisation. In this sense, emotional pain experienced by workers as a by-product of everyday organisational life can be seen as a pathological phenomenon in that it is 'dysfunctional, damaging and painful for organizations' (Gabriel, 2012:1138), and yet it is inflicted by practices within the organisations. This paradoxical quality of emotional pain and toxicity continues to remain unspoken and hidden, in part because of the emotional labour gifted by those who undertake the work of the toxin handler.

Appreciating the vital role toxin handlers play in alleviating emotional wear and tear on both the organisations and individuals in pain, either informally or formally, gives rise to a number of interesting and related questions. For example, to what extent do we all absorb toxin-handling responsibilities throughout an organisation? What differentiates those who can handle toxins from those who cannot? It is to this second question that we now turn as we look to the work of Bourdieu to develop the concept of emotional capital to help us explore why some of us are willing to undertake and even enjoy work that others of us appear unable to do.

6 Emotional capital

Exposure, experience and praxis

'It's never affected me. It's never affected me, never. It doesn't bother me at all, what they do or how much I have got to clean up. . . . You know, you just do it. It's part of your job.'

(Janice, home care worker)

Many of us would recoil at the thought of listening to a paedophile explore his feelings, or making a decision to euthanize someone's beloved pet cat or being required to show restraint in the face of violence, but for some doing so is a routine and everyday part of work life. In setting out to write this book, we interviewed a range of people who worked in a variety of often emotionally challenging occupations that often involve some kind of emotionally difficult or dirty work (Hughes, 1958; McMurray & Ward, 2014). What became apparent was that many of those we interviewed seemed to take their work and its challenges in their stride. As Vera noted at the beginning of Chapter 4, it is the kind of work that some people can do 'and some people can't' (Vera, home care worker). In this chapter we consider what enables some people to cope with the dark side of emotional labour while others cannot.

Why do we each have different reactions, tolerances and capacities to perform emotional labour, and why is it that we differ in our ability to thrive in different emotional 'fields' (Bourdieu, 1977)? Our task is to consider the nature of the practices, experiences and related resources drawn upon by workers in the course of emotional performances 'on the dark side' to better understand the nature, texture and lived experiences of those who work in extreme emotional contexts (Zembylas, 2007) and to make rigorous observations about life experiences that may have contributed to their ability to undertake such work. The questions we then seek to raise – and encourage others to pursue – are twofold: do different life experiences predispose different people to undertake work in particular emotional contexts, and, relatedly, do those experiences mean that some people are better equipped to cope with the light and dark that accompany emotional labour? The remainder of this chapter begins to tackle these crucial questions by introducing, defining and exploring the concept of 'emotional capital'. Through analysis of spoken accounts of emotion at work, we are able to identify three key factors in the development of emotional capital: exposure, experience and praxis. We also note that emotional capital (and its accumulation) suggests a process of learning in respect of coping with and performing emotional labour. While this suggestion of learning has been popularised by the very narrow literature on emotional intelligence, we have in mind a broader, more socially embedded understanding of learning as socialisation.[1]

We start by defining what we mean by emotional capital. Drawing on Bourdieu's typology of capital, we consider how an additional category that centralises the emotions might usefully inform our understanding of why we each have different capacities and abilities to perform emotional labour and cope in different emotional contexts, particularly those that are dark, uncomfortable and challenging. A review of the extant literature on emotional capital reveals that theorisation of the concept and its application as an analytical tool have taken place almost exclusively within the field of educational research (Zembylas, 2007; Reay, 2004, 2000; O'Brien, 2008; Gillies, 2006; exceptions include Cahill, 1999; Probyn, 2004). Whilst these debates and illustrations of the concept are both thought provoking and illuminating, they are heavily laden with normative assumptions of middle-class practices, attitudes and moralities, which is a well-rehearsed critique of Bourdieu's work. Responding to Zembylas's (2007:452) call to extend the 'use of emotional capital to other fields besides parental involvement or women's roles', we contend that emotional capital has been a marginalised factor in understanding why some people can work on the dark side and others cannot. Our analysis of interview data extracts from veterinarians, bereavement counsellors, home care workers and Samaritans follows Hughes (1984) in that our attempt is to illustrate the connections between the life experiences of those in different occupational groups, paying particular attention to the choice and the capacity to perform emotional labour. We start, then, by turning to Bourdieu's account of 'forms of capital' with a view to positioning an additional manifestation in the form of emotional capital.

Bourdieu's forms of capital

Pierre Bourdieu's conceptual framework of 'capital' is premised on the idea that 'the social world is accumulated history' (Bourdieu, 1986:241). For Bourdieu, capital is accumulated labour that exists in either a material or an embodied form and that can present itself in a variety of guises; economic, social, cultural and symbolic. The term 'capital' is used in its widest sense in that it refers to 'all the goods, material and symbolic, without distinction, that present themselves as rare and worthy of being sought after in a particular social formation' (Harker *et al.*, 1990:1).

Economic capital is that which has direct exchange value and therefore can be converted into money (e.g. inheritance, income or property rights). Social capital is the value created via social relationships, connections and networks (e.g. reputation, affiliate memberships, title). Cultural capital is a little more complex in that this type of capital is given value and meaning through social and institutional discourse (e.g. qualifications, league tables, brands). Finally, then, symbolic capital is 'the form that the various species of capital assume when they are perceived and recognized as legitimate' (Bourdieu, 1989:17). Symbolic capital is not an additional form of capital to economic, social and cultural but is a representation of an existing form of capital that has undergone 'conversion' to become 'legitimate' and therefore has accumulated power, prestige and honour. Such 'legitimacy' is typically enshrined and defined by middle-class values (Gillies, 2006).

'Emotional capital' was not a term explicitly used or developed by Bourdieu. In fact, Bourdieu's treatment of emotion is extremely vague and is often implicitly associated with women's work (Reay, 2000; and see Probyn, 2004 for a detailed account of Bourdieu's position on emotion), as is so often the case in academic studies of emotion (see Chapter 2).

Nowotny (1981), in one of the first attempts to extend the notion of capital, sees emotional capital as a gendered variant of social capital operating within the private sphere in that it is a product of the affective social relationships of family and friends and refers to 'Knowledge, contacts and relations as well as access to emotionally valued skills and assets, which hold within any social network, characterised at least partly by affective ties' (Nowotny, 1981:148). Nowotny's claim that emotional capital is a 'resource women have in greater abundance than men' (Reay, 2000:572) sets a gendered agenda of research for the concept, with the majority of subsequent studies focusing on the ways in which mothers devote their skills and resources to the advancement of their children, particularly in an educational context. Moreover, the resulting studies have predominantly involved a comparative analysis of middle-class and working-class mothers' emotional capital 'investment' techniques (see Gillies, 2006; Reay, 2000, 2004; Allatt, 1993; see Manion, 2007, for an international comparison). These studies have focused on the ways in which families (i.e. mothers) generate this type of capital in the form of 'emotionally valued assets and skill, love and affection, expenditure of time, attention, care and concern' (Allatt, 1993:143). Yet, what these studies seem to have overlooked is Bourdieu's most basic definition of capital 'as accumulated history'. Each of the studies cited has a microlevel focus on the behaviours and parenting techniques of individual mothers but fails to include a discussion of those mother's life histories, upbringing and experiences or, indeed, a discussion of the impact that these emotional-capital building techniques are having on those in whom they are being invested (i.e. their children) and their choices. For Bourdieu, life and capital are temporal and dynamic rather than static; they are built, understood and shaped over time. The impact of capital is ever changing, as learning (in the widest possible sense) is a process of becoming, manifest and experienced through a system of dispositions ('habitus') and within specific social and cultural contexts ('fields').

In many ways, the construction of emotional capital as a gendered capital (Reay, 2004) and the microlevel focus on parenting techniques have, in our mind and that of others (Zembylas, 2007; Colley *et al.*, 2007), stunted the development and operationalisation of the concept. Responding to Zembylas's (2007:455) call for a broader definition of emotional capital 'as investments that have significant social, cultural and economic implications' that are not restricted by gender or class, we turn back to Bourdieu's concepts of 'field' and 'habitus' to explore the idea of emotional capital as a socially, culturally and economically informed capacity to labour emotionally. Such an alternative definition seeks to explain why there are 'those who can cope and those who can't cope' with dark emotions.

Emotional capital

Nowotny (1981) and Allatt (1993) have both attempted to define emotional capital. In many ways, defining such a concept risks reducing it to something which is manageable, containable and therefore exploitable, which runs counter to Bourdieu's own treatment of the other forms of capital. For Bourdieu, the complexity and interrelated nature of each of the forms of capital prevents a single, neat definition of each of the concepts. In many ways this is evident in existing attempts to define emotional capital. Each has its flaws and omissions and fails to encapsulate the extent to which emotions are socially, culturally, economically and psychologically formed, informed and performed.

> knowledge, contacts and relations as well as access to emotionally valued skills and assets, which hold within any social network characterized at least partly by affective ties
>
> (Nowotny, 1981:148)

> emotionally valued assets and skill, love and affection, expenditure of time, attention, care and concern
>
> (Allatt, 1993:143)

Whilst Nowotny's attempt is more generic and usefully reflects the influence of the 'field', the generative and dynamic character of emotional capital is not mentioned, and neither are the individual, biographical experiences that inform the habitus. By privileging care and empathy, Allatt's definition is firmly embedded within the middle-class values espoused by Bourdieu and institutionalised by social rhetoric. The possibility that skills, habits and capacities can be usefully drawn from 'the dark side' – from experiences of fear, disgust, exposure and Otherness – is excluded. Reay (2000:569) states that she has utilised emotional capital as a 'heuristic device [rather] than an overarching conceptual framework'. This is something we too feel more comfortable with as it reflects Bourdieu's own approach to working through his ideas and theoretical conceptualisations. However, our presentation of emotional capital attempts to reflect its inherent complexity, multifaceted, generative and longitudinal nature, whilst also illustrating the ways in which emotional capital separates those who can from those who can't. In this way we tentatively define emotional capital *as 'the capacity to perceive, perform and manage contextually relevant emotions (where such capacity is) acquired through exposure, experience and praxis'.*

Arguably, emotional capital cannot be understood without an appreciation of Bourdieu's most central concepts of 'habitus' and 'field'. As we touched upon earlier, 'habitus' is best thought of as a 'system of dispositions' (Bourdieu, 1977). These dispositions are a spectrum of cognitive and affective factors (see Probyn, 2004) that constitute a 'product of history [that] produces individual and collective practices' (Bourdieu, 1990:54). It is perhaps already apparent that even this foundational definition of one of Bourdieu's key concepts stands in opposition to the methodological and analytical approaches of much of the education literature in the area of emotional capital. Much of this literature focuses on individual-level accounts that are effectively snapshots of mothers' emotional dispositions in relation to their child's educational performance. Yet, arguably, to encapsulate the extent to which the habitus is an 'embodied history, internalised as second nature and so forgotten' (Bourdieu, 1990:56), there is sense in suggesting a more biographical, ethnographic approach may offer fruitful insights into that which has become second nature. In other words, habitus is a dynamic and generative embodied manifestation of prior experiences that will (though not conclusively or even predictably) influence behaviours, emotions and frames of reference.

Bourdieu's other significant foundational concept is that of field. 'Field' is in essence context – 'discourses, institutions, values, rules and regulations – which produce and transform attitudes and practices'(Webb *et al.*, 2013:21). Each social context has its own rules and norms which influence and shape (in)appropriate behaviours and feelings. Drawing on Ekman's (1973) concept of display rules, Hochschild (1979) developed 'feeling rules' to explain the ways in which we self-regulate our emotional response even in a private context (e.g. we might feel guilty for not feeling sad at a funeral or happy at a party because our personal disposition is somewhat at odds with the prevalent feeling rule of that particular context). However, just because feeling rules and emotion norms might exist, this does not mean that they are fixed; neither do they exclusively determine behaviour. Instead, they are there to guide: they are the rules of the game, but this does not mean that the rules are never broken or rewritten.

Emotional capital, then, as well as being an investment in resources at a microlevel, as it has been presented in the education literature, is, perhaps more importantly, a form of capital that shapes identity, occupational choice and a capacity to emotionally labour – in some cases on the 'dark side'. Our past experiences, as well as our gender and class, shape who we are, creating our individual habitus. This habitus is neither definitive nor static but is instead open ended and continually renegotiated as we encounter new experiences that challenge our perceived notion of self and Other, with the politics of difference informing who we are, how we see ourselves and our positions within the 'fields' that we occupy.

On this basis we argue that emotional capital is a result of a cumulative process of becoming (without end), the construction and application of which is context dependent. In what follows we consider how emotional capital is accumulated through *exposure*, *experience* and *praxis*.

Emotional capital and emotional labour

The ability of Bourdieu's forms of capital to be 'converted' from one form to another is a key aspect of his theory. Where emotional capital has been operationalised in the education literature, there has been almost no consideration of emotional capital's ability to convert into other forms. What is particularly relevant to the relationship between emotional capital and emotional labour is one of Bourdieu's paradoxical observations:

> it has to be posited simultaneously that economic capital is at the root of all the other types of capital and that these transformed, disguised forms of economic capital, never entirely reducible to that definition, produce their most specific effects only to the extent that they conceal the fact that economic capital is at their root.
>
> (Bourdieu, 1986:252)

The ability to smile at just the right time, show deference in particular situations and exercise discretion and modesty in complex relational encounters allows us to construct a particular version of ourselves that has social capital that is easily converted into cultural capital, assuming we know the social and emotional rules of the encounter. The ability to read the feeling norms and display rules associated with a given 'field' allows us to convert that emotional capital into social capital; for example, a person schooled and practiced in the personal and professional emotional tone required during 'after-work drinks' increases her chances of being welcomed into particular social networks (private and public, personal and professional). In turn, these networks can serve to facilitate career progression (most controversially through the 'old boys' network); thus, emotional capital, in the form of emotion management, leads to an accumulation of economic capital. Interestingly, Nowotny's (1981) initial presentation of emotional capital (which preceded the publication of Hochschild's *The Managed Heart*) failed to appreciate its links to economic capital:

> The rules of the labour market are such that emotional capital gained in the private sphere is not convertible into economic capital, for this exchange relationship has long been depersonalized, and private capital is of little value in the outside world. This means that emotional capital which is valueless in the public sphere is largely used for further investments in children and (especially upwardly mobile) husbands.
>
> (Nowotny, 1981:148)

To be clear, emotional labour was presented by Hochschild (1983) with its root in Marxist thinking as a commodification of what were once personal emotions into publicly saleable commodities. Hochschild's (1983) major contribution to the work on emotion was to assert that in fact emotions have both exchange value and use value. In other words, emotions have an economic value. In relation to Bourdieu, then, Hochschild's contribution makes a foundational step in asserting that emotions have the ability to operate as a form of capital. The now extensive body of literature that has followed Hochschild illustrates a range of occupations that involve some kind of emotional labour, from the cabin crew paid to smile and calm passengers to our own work with door staff paid to intimidate. In each case, certain types of emotional performance are a central job requirement and, as such, are of economic value. Emotional performances are therefore traded even though their precise economic value and root may be concealed.

This last point takes us back to Bourdieu's paradox – not only does each form of capital have to be rooted in economic capital but all forms 'produce their most specific effects' (Bourdieu, 1986:252) when their economic origin is concealed. Emotional labour is most effective when the performance generated appears to be genuine. As consumers, we want to feel that the customer service representative really does care about us as a consumer, while often shying away from the acknowledgement that a moment of humour, empathy or servility is part of a marketised exchange. From the perspective of the client (and employer), the specific and valued effect of emotional labour is the concealment of its exchange value. Such concealment might arise from the convincing display of deep acting offered by the worker and accepted by the client, or there may be mutual collusion in the surface denial of a forced, scripted or tacitly required emotional performance and response.

Considered thus as concealed value, emotional labour is often to be found on the darker side of organisational life. For some this darker side of their work is an unwelcome by-product of the tasks they undertake. For others they are the very essence of their work – the raison d'être and occupational calling. But what is it that makes this difference, this distinction? The possibility that our social, cultural and prior experiences shape our capacities to frame, construct and cope with difficult occupational challenges is one that moves us away from essentialist ideas that certain people are inherently suited to particular jobs and towards a situated perspective that raises the possibility that our life experiences, upbringing, educational socialisation and organisational culture continually shape our emotional capacities (Colley *et al.*, 2007). It invites us to construct an account of emotional capital by drawing the there-then into the here-now: by inviting workers who work on the dark side to consider how and why they have arrived at their present position. It is through the lenses of exposure, experience and praxis that we present the accounts of those who undertake work on the dark side to illustrate the ways in which they feel their capacity to undertake such work has been and continues to be acquired and developed and the specific effects that arise from the deployment of such capital. We start with accounts of exposure.

Exposure

> I kept lots of pets as a kid. My parents had a small-holding. I didn't think I could cope with blood until, on a Boxing Day, I went out with a vet to a horse that was haemorrhaging badly from its nose and he just happened to be with us on Boxing Day, and, yes, never looked back.
>
> (Jack, veterinary surgeon)

With more than 20 years of veterinary practice under his belt, Jack owes a lot to that one seemingly random opportunity that saw him accompany a vet on a dramatic call-out. Jack's story offers comment on the situatedness of his occupational choice. Growing up on a small-holding provided him with the space and resource to keep 'lots of pets', something that would not be true of a child growing up in an inner-city flat. Bourdieu might argue that Jack's childhood was one that gave him access to a variety of forms of capital, equipping him with resources to make his occupational choice (economic – paying for a veterinary degree; social – having a relationship with a vet who encouraged his involvement; cultural – social networks that validated his desire to become a vet). And yet, this one single childhood experience stands out for Jack as being irrevocably influential. So, although we can read economic, cultural and social capital into this narrative, predominantly as a consequence of class, it is important not to overlook the emotional sense-making processes that were also taking place. The emotional capital accumulated in that moment (i.e. the knowledge that he had the capacity to manage his emotional reaction to the sight of blood) contributed to his choosing to practice veterinary medicine.

Something similar is recalled in Cahill's (1999) participative observation of mortuary science students. Cahill revealed that professional socialisation was built upon preexisting socialisation or exposure that students brought with them to the course. In many cases this was in the form of having been raised in and around funeral homes and other occupations that exposed the students to death and work with the dead. This 'prior socialisation' had allowed them to master any 'fear of death and revulsion' (Cahill, 1999:112) that such work might evoke, thus equipping them with the emotional capacity and resources that would then be refined via professional training and practice. For those of us who lack such experience, the critically acclaimed American TV series *Six Feet Under* (2001–2005) subtly narrates starkly contrasting perspectives and reactions towards death and, in particular, dead bodies in a Los Angeles funeral home. For clients and mourners, the body is something that is 'presented' formally and ritualistically in an open casket, not to be touched but to be gazed upon in reverence. For the Fisher family, who live and work in the funeral home, death is about a body which, while treated respectfully, represents work and income. The family are intimately acquainted with the work that has taken place to make the 'viewing' of the body possible, work that often involves reconstructive surgical techniques, embalming and hours of contact with the body and bodily fluids. The skill of the family is in rendering this work invisible to mourners. Lifelong exposure to such contact ensures that the worker's emotions are measured and contained, in respect not just of their physically dirty work with bodies but also of the emotional dirty work of dealing with the bereaved. Exposure therefore contributes to the development of the emotional capital required to maintain the rituals, performances and presentations that are required in respect of death and burial. It is this developing familial (and the vocational) habitus (Smith & Kleinman, 1989; Colley *et al.*, 2007) that helps to explain why some individuals are more likely than others to be able to stomach such work. As Cahill notes:

> there are good reasons to suspect that the extent, timing and sequence of children's exposure to different emotions, to evaluations of particular emotions, and to feeling and expression rules varies by social class, parental occupation, ethnicity and gender.
>
> (Cahill, 1999:112)

Cahill's (1999) point about parental occupation is particularly pertinent to the three generations of home care workers we interviewed for this book. Generational interviewing encourages those involved to explore how various but linked experiences evolved and have been differentially experienced and interpreted over time. For younger workers the chance to interact with older generations invites consideration of formative experiences that, until now, may not have been explicitly discussed or explained. From our perspective they open up the possibility of constructing more nuanced accounts of occupational trajectories as well as the processes through which emotional capital is accumulated and transferred in familial/occupational settings. Take for example this account of early socialisation in home care work:

> Janice: 'I used to take Caroline with me . . . down to Wood House when it first opened and she absolutely hated the old people.'
> Caroline: 'I was about four or five.'
> Janice: 'They used to open their handbags and take out a sweet covered in fluff, ooh, a wrinkled old apple, and the look on her face! I used to say to her just accept it and give it to me and I will get rid of it, because I said you will hurt their feelings. She was fascinated by false teeth.'
> Caroline: 'They scared me! . . . It scared me to death when I was little so I was quite surprised when I did give it a go – I only went in to it because I needed the money – so I gave it a go and I loved it. I have never looked back. . . . So, although the money is rubbish there is definitely job satisfaction.'
>
> (Janice and Caroline, home care workers)

Not only are these three generations of women intriguing in relation to emotional capital but their presentation of Caroline's early socialisation, or exposure, into the home care setting is imbued with emotionality and with evidence of her being taught the 'rules of the game', the feeling rules and emotion norms (Hochschild, 1979) or, as Bourdieu would have it, the 'field' and 'habitus'. Specifically, Janice recounts instructing Caroline to behave in particular ways so as to account for the feelings of the elderly whilst Caroline herself recalls her emotional reactions of fascination and fear. These darker emotions experienced by Caroline may well have deterred her from pursuing this occupation herself. Indeed, the extract suggests that her initial involvement revolved around financial need but that ultimately she 'loved it' and continues to undertake the work despite the fact that the 'money is rubbish'.

Caroline recounts how subsequent training in dealing with people with dementia, Parkinson's and stroke and the associated techniques and medication have all contributed to the emotional habitus of the home care worker. But she also leaves us in little doubt that it was her formative experiences as a child and her continued association with older generations of home carers that prepared her to undertake and gain satisfaction from such challenging occupational work. By contrast, she notes that many new young recruits do not last:

> Caroline: 'We have young girls, I wouldn't say just coming out of school but we have young girls of 18 doing it.'
> Jenna: 'And do you think they're prepared for what they have to do?'
> Caroline: 'I doubt it to be honest, I doubt it. No I wouldn't have thought so. It's probably a bit of a shock for them. We have quite a large turnover of staff so they don't last long. Yeah, there are not many of us

where I am now that's been there [a long time], we have been there quite a long time a few of us.'

Jenna: 'Do you think that's because you have grown up with it [home care work]?'

Caroline: Yeah,'

(Caroline, home care worker)

These examples of working with animals, home care residents and death speak to the way in which childhood experiences or prior socialisation manifest as emotional capital acquired through exposure. However, this is not to say that all childhood exposures lead to positive emotional capital; many people are left traumatised by certain experiences and carry the emotional impact with them for the rest of their lives. Furthermore, we are not suggesting that childhood and upbringing are the only opportunities for emotional capital building. As Colley *et al.* (2007:488) argue, 'predisposition is necessary [but] it is not sufficient'. Following Bourdieu's broadest definition of capital as 'accumulated histories', we look to other life experiences and praxis via professional socialisation as additional and dynamic forms of emotional capital.

Experience

So far, we have illustrated the extent to which emotional capital can be acquired through exposure to particular emotions of relevance to the 'field' and seen how acquisitions to the emotional habitus can be used to generate professional opportunities and even affect career choice. Another source of capital building identified in our analysis stemmed from the very frank and open discussions with those who volunteer to provide emotional support as Samaritans. Frank's and Brian's poignant honesty provides us with an insight into the ways in which life experiences, both past and present, construct value systems and dispositions towards those in emotional crisis. They have lived through, even survived in many ways, their own individual emotional traumas, and the 'knowledge' (as habitus) they have acquired has shaped their perception of the 'lived experience' of others. The personal life experiences of both of these Samaritans mean that they now view the emotions and behaviors of others, including suicide, suicidal thoughts and depression in perhaps a different way to the broader discourse within mainstream society, where suicide might be deemed by some as cowardly and selfish and mental health issues may be seen as less 'legitimate' concerns than ills that pertain to the physical body. Frank's and Brian's life experiences have manifest in a naturalised habitus – unconscious perception and sense-making, if you will:

When I got married my wife had got a child and that was putting a bit of pressure on us and then we had a couple of kids and . . . I did quite well workwise and earned a lot of money. But err . . . it became quite intolerable, the situation and . . . I was in a bad way and if I could have gone off the Baketon Bridge I would have done. . . . I think without their help [Samaritans] I would not be here today, I am sure I would have jumped . . . sadly my eldest son he died at 32 years of age, 3 and a half years ago . . . there is a lot of people in those positions, there is more than you think when you start talking to colleagues in work or in your private life. . . . And we live in a world where everything has got to be glossy, we have got to be strong . . . but we are not, we are human beings. We have our own frailties . . . we all have a yearning for a bit of love and understanding.

(Frank, Samaritan)

I have suffered from depression for a long time . . . its affected me quite badly. Urm . . . mostly over the last ten years but a lot before that. . . . I didn't realise what was really happening. . . . I was sort of wandering through life trying to get back . . . so the last sort of ten years I haven't really worked very much, I have taken a lot of medications . . . spent a lot of time not engaging with anything or anyone . . . a lot of the people who call [Samaritans] . . . have got very similar experiences to me . . . so I find empathising with people who are really struggling or kind of like outsiders, I find that quite easy. I find the non-judgemental side of it very easy now as well because I know how easy it is to get messed up in a way that people on the outside will not understand.

(Brian, Samaritan)

Both Frank and Brian bring their emotional experiences to their work for Samaritans. The experience of depression, the experience of family tensions, the experience of suicidal thoughts and the knowledge of being helped by Samaritans inform their labours with others. Their personal emotional experiences mean that they 'find empathising with people who are really struggling . . . quite easy' (Brian), and they appreciate that 'we have our own frailties . . . we all have a yearning for a bit of love and understanding' (Frank).

Their own life experiences led to a capacity to empathise with certain Samaritan callers. They have been touched by or experienced emotions and, just as important, experienced a working through of those emotions, in a way that others of us have not. Such encounters and their ability to survive emboldened these individuals to seek out work and activities that bring them in proximity to feelings and emotions that once consumed them. These wider life experiences have increased their individual ability to understand particular emotional relations and to respond to the demands that those relations imply.

This suggests a certain durability of the habitus in the manner by Webb *et al.* (2013:41) in that:

dispositions, knowledges and values are always potentially subject to modification, rather than being passively consumed or reinscribed. This occurs when the narratives, values and explanations of a habitus no longer make sense . . . when agents use their understanding and feel for the rules of the game as a means of furthering or improving their own standing and capital within a cultural field. It must be stressed, however, that such 'interests' are themselves produced by, and through the habitus.

In other words, and perhaps a little pessimistically, Frank's and Brian's habitus has been subject to modification to improve their own standing. Specifically, their standing is altered by the act of reframing their personal experiences as something valuable insofar as it can be useful in helping others. Through their work as Samaritans, they are able to move beyond those personally traumatic experiences, such that emotional experience becomes emotional competence. As Illouz (1997:56) argues:

> the ability to distance oneself from one's immediate emotional experience is the prerogative of those who have readily available a range of emotional options, who are not overwhelmed by emotional necessity and intensity and can therefore approach their own self and emotions with the same detached mode that comes from accumulated emotional competence.

For Illouz (1997), this ability to distance oneself from the immediacy of a situation is a product of *'accumulated emotional competence'* or, alternatively, 'emotional capital'. This is not to say that Frank and Brian now have sufficient emotional capital to be unaffected by any call they receive. In fact, encounters with callers often force Samaritans to stand at the precipice of their own emotional frailty, to challenge themselves each and every time the telephone rings, as Kate testifies:

> I had a sister who tragically died from breast cancer very young and so if I get a call exactly like that I will be very aware, watch it, don't start thinking about your sister.
>
> (Kate, Samaritan)

Each call, each emotional encounter, then builds on the emotional capital they have already acquired into their habitus, whether from prior socialisation, professional socialisation in parallel or previous careers, or their own personal life experiences – allowing them to endure and even enjoy work that provokes others to ask, 'Why would you want to do that?' (see Chapter 4).

Samaritans and those in other occupations do offer an interesting counterpoint to thinking around the conversion of forms of capital. Although the ability to listen to and empathise with those who are in emotional distress or are confessing to inappropriate behaviours or feelings is a valued occupational capital within the 'field' of the Samaritan organisation, this does not mean that this capital is appreciated or valued in the same way outside the organisation. A Samaritan's commitment to self-determination (a core tenet of the service the organisation provides), for example, is praised within the organisational community; however, the ability to stand back and let another person harm himself (e.g. to neither condemn nor condone an active suicide attempt) is not necessarily a trait that would be perceived in a positive light in any other social context. In this sense, Samaritans' occupationally valued emotional capital is not necessarily easily converted into social capital because it stands in stark contrast to the dominant emotionology (Stearns & Stearns, 1985) surrounding death and care. This problematic juxtaposition of norms and rules ('fields') may offer some insight into why certain occupational contexts have the ability to taint or stigmatise those who engage with it (see Chapter 4).

Praxis

Bates (1991) argues that a person's suitability for undertaking particular types of work is constructed both culturally and socially. We have demonstrated, in support of this position, that, for our participants who work with challenging, uncomfortable and disruptive emotions, their suitability for this work has indeed been informed by past exposures and experiences that were a product of their situation both socially and culturally.

However, this is not to imply that the dramatic events of a Boxing Day or his upbringing on a small-holding equipped Jack with *all* of the emotional capital he would need to work and deal with the often dark reality of being a veterinarian. Typically you might think that 'darkness' in veterinary work involves cases of animal cruelty or euthanasia (Sanders, 2010). And yet, for Jack, as has been detailed elsewhere (see Sanders, 2010), dealing with his own emotions and those of his clients is perhaps more challenging:

> I can cope with that side of it [euthanasia] because I know I'm doing it for the animal and at the end of the day I'm stopping the animal suffering . . . the bit that gets to me and I have, yes, I've been teary at times, is when it's their [pet owner's] sole companion . . . and the teariness . . . is not for the animal but it's the person that's left behind . . . it's their whole world and so you're taking that away.

Feelings of failure and frustration were also attributed to the 'dark side' of the work:

> if you can't help someone's animal you feel a failure . . . if you know there is absolutely no chance, you know, it's got cancer and it's inevitable, fair enough, but if you can't get a diagnosis to make it better then you start feeling inadequate almost . . . the other is when . . . you've done everything right but the client thinks you haven't and you're in the

wrong as far as the client is aware . . . because they are thinking about their baby they are not listening . . . but yes that will often eat me when I go home and I feel you haven't quite done it right, but knowing that actually you had no control.

At the time when Jack undertook his formal veterinarian training, the programme did not include any aspect of client management or how to cope with the darker, more challenging aspects of the role. Instead this knowledge has been something Jack has developed over time, through observation of himself and others and by trial and error, via professional socialisation or that which Colley *et al.* (2007) term 'vocational habitus'. In other words, this emotional capital was gained through engagement with and negation of specific situations, feelings and approaches, that is, praxis. For Friere (1992), praxis is the action and reflection upon practice which has the potential to lead to transformation. For Jack, this combination of action and reflection is clearly something he sees as key in building the emotional capital required of veterinary work:

> We had no training 20 years ago about that [coping and managing emo-tions] . . . but I still don't think it [would] help you cope with it. Seeing practice does because you see how different vets . . . react in different ways . . . so really it is only seeing practice.

Interestingly, Jack's use of the term 'practice' here refers to the exercise or activities of the profession of veterinary work, and yet it also encourages us to consider the extent to which observing and actively participating in (i.e. practicing) the complex reality of coping with and managing the emotions of self and other becomes habitual or, in Bourdieu's sense of the word, part of the individual 'habitus' – a capacity – emotional capital.

Similarly for Denise, who had undertaken a year-long distance learning course to become a pet bereavement counsellor, the content of the course had focused on the feelings of the bereaved and strategies for their coping rather than on the impact interactions with these difficult emotions would have on those undertaking this work. However, Denise's work with diffi-cult and challenging emotions is not an unhealthy, unwanted by-product of other work but the focus of what she does, what drives and motivates her to continue doing her job. This is her occupational calling and has been a feature of her previous employments:

> Well it's really weird because before I had the kids I was involved with care work anyway, and I did a lot of terminal illness. Again, it's been a side of me that is just, I don't know what it is about it but I enjoy helping people through grief, because I think I have got a lot to give on that.
>
> (Denise, pet bereavement counsellor)

Arguably, the care work Denise undertook prior to her becoming a pet bereavement counsellor gave her exposure and access to 'caring in practice' – praxis. She intimates that this ability to 'remove' herself has been something she has crafted 'over the years' – in other words, through action and reflection (praxis), she has learnt to distance herself from the immediacy of the grief and trauma whilst still being able to provide emotional support. This distance acquired through praxis and practice gives her the capacity to manage both her own emotions and those of the person for whom she is caring:

> putting to sleep has got to be fairly traumatic . . . I would say *not so much for me anymore because I came to terms with it over the years dealing with people* and I just . . . I don't go through the emotions, I still feel it, but it's become very much part of my job and it is just part of my role . . . it's not that I don't feel it because I do feel people's, you know, their grief. It's terrible. But I think actually removing myself from it a little bit helps me be able to deal with it a little better. So they get a better, a more positive response.
>
> (Denise, pet bereavement counsellor, emphasis added)

But perhaps Denise's 'calling' for bereavement work is something that can be traced back to earlier events in her life, as prior 'experience'. In a fleeting comment towards the end of her interview she remarked:

> you do beat yourself up about it but there is nothing you can do . . . it's gone. The same as our Springer Spaniel . . . when he died . . . she [Mum] didn't come out of her bedroom for four days . . . we were putting her drinks by the door. She was in a hell of a state. I have never seen anyone grieve like that.
>
> (Denise, pet bereavement counsellor)

For Denise, then, we can see that her capacity to work so closely with such intense grief on a daily basis (emotional capital) and for much of her working life has been acquired over time through an interplay of exposure, experience and praxis. This is something Bourdieu refers to as the principle of regulated improvisation (1977:78). The 'habitus' is informed, at least in part, by our unconscious absorption of values and dispositions which remain with us across contexts, thereby making them both durable and transposable. The durability and transposability of these values and dispositions allow for effective improvisations whereby we use the knowledge of the habitus and the 'rules of the game' (the field) to respond in a dynamic and sensitive way.

Anthony, too, could see some clear parallels in the emotional work of being a Samaritan and his previous occupation as a solicitor:

> Perhaps . . . if I tell you a little bit about the mental health work I was doing . . . I was representing people with schizophrenia and things like

that . . . and so consequently I had, unfortunately, I had several of my clients commit suicide. I saw desperately sad people but I could understand why one or two of them did it because this was a life that for them . . . it was no, no, no life. . . . (pause) A bipolar teacher killed herself and I could understand, I had represented her for many years and I could understand why eventually she was going to kill herself.

(Anthony, retired solicitor and Samaritan)

This interplay among exposure, experience and praxis as emotional capital accumulation is not only being used in organisational contexts for organisational ends. Emotional capital generated through occupational praxis can also become a powerful resource to be drawn upon in a personal context. Janice recounts how she, her daughter and her granddaughter (all of whom work as carers) cared for her late mother at home despite her incontinence:

Something wasn't right with her bowels and . . . she couldn't control her bowels and that was it you know. And it's my mum I am having to do this for. . . . And I used to make her laugh, I used to say to her 'Aren't you glad I didn't go into banking?'. . . 'I would run a mile!'. . . Caroline would sort her out when I was trying to work . . . and Sophie was good with her Nan.

(Janice, home care worker)

In recounting this touching memory of joking with her incontinent mother to put her at her ease as she 'sorts her out', Janice is actually illustrating an interesting point about the way in which emotional capital is not categorised or compartmentalised into public or private, use or exchange value. Here, Janice, Caroline and Sophie all drew on their preexisting capital that had been, at least in part, acquired through prolonged professional and prior socialisation in the care of their mother, grandmother and great grandmother in a respectful, professional and caring way.

These experiences and exposures to various fields of emotional complexity have been embodied or, in Bourdieu's vocabulary of capital, 'acquired' by the emotional habitus or system of dispositions. They are opportunities for reflection and transformation that these individuals would not have had had they not been working in these particular occupations. These occupational experiences have generated 'emotional perceptions, reactions, expressions and emotion management strategies' (Cahill, 1999:112) that the workers have gone on to use in different occupational contexts and emotional 'fields', illustrating the generative capacity of emotional capital and the principle of regulated improvisations.

Conclusion

In this chapter we have explored the extent to which the 'acquisition and accumulation' of emotional capital might differentiate those who can from those who cannot in relation to undertaking certain types of emotional labour in certain contexts, particularly those labouring on the 'dark side'. Drawing on a small but growing body of work from education studies on emotional capital, we followed Cahill's (1999) lead in exploring the impact emotional capital has on building emotional capacities.

We do not claim that the absence of specific exposures, experiences or praxis inevitably precludes individuals from particular types of emotional labour. However, the testimonies of Jack, Caroline, Janice, Denise, Kate and Anthony do suggest that the development of emotional capital can facilitate the execution of and even excellence in certain types of emotion work. It helps explain 'why they would want to do that'. It reveals that the acquisition of emotional capital is a generative and iterative process gained from prior socialisation through upbringing, birthright, gender and class. Such capital is accumulated throughout our lives as we encounter and negotiate all of life's trial and tribulations (some more extreme than others). It is developed and honed via professional socialisation as we continually use, re-use and renegotiate how those experiences shape our habitus, our system of dispositions, our way of looking at the world and what we can and cannot cope with. Thus, we posit that a broader conceptualisation of emotional capital, one that includes the iterative, generative and dynamic influence of life experience and childhood upbringing, along with the traditionally cited gender and class, effectively creates individual emotional dispositions ('habitus') that renders each of us with the emotional capacity to be drawn to, enact and thrive in particular emotional contexts ('fields').

The ability to work on the 'dark side' has much to do with the emotional capital we have acquired from our accumulated history, how we live and experience new encounters and how those new experiences tessellate with those that have gone before. For some, this equips them with an ability to undertake some of the most challenging types of work, while for others it means that they are less well suited. Given the relative paucity of work across disciplines on emotional capital, we hope that this chapter serves as a wellspring of ideas and further research into the nature, methods of acquisition and consequences of emotional capital as a factor in the capacity to perform certain types of emotional labour.

Finally, on the basis that we argue emotional capital to be a result of a cumulative process of becoming (without end), the construction and application of which is context dependent, we call for empirical research into emotional capital to look beyond traditional methods of semistructured interviewing. In his text *The Weight of the World?* (1999) Bourdieu advocates a more self-reflexive approach to research, claiming that one essential strategy in this approach is for 'interviewers to have an extensive knowledge of the social contexts of their subjects . . . as a result of having a 'history of interviewing the same interviewee' (Webb *et al.*, 2013:55–56). Perhaps methods such as biographical narrative interviewing, longitudinal and intergenerational studies and ethnographic approaches would allow for an in-depth qualitative appreciation of the 'accumulated [emotional] history' (Bourdieu, 1977) of self that manifests as emotional capital.

Note

1 It is important to point out here that we are not seeking to identify why certain people can do work that others cannot as a managerialist or functionalist call for better emotional control or an improvement in emotional intelligence (Mayer and Salovey, 1997). Rather, we are concerned to develop a more sociological understanding of how it is that individuals accumulate or build the internal resources required to undertake and cope with the dark side of emotional labour in the first place. Such an understanding may offer benefits in the recruitment of those who are more likely to cope and/or identify those in need of greater support.

7 Emotional labour and the ethics of care

'THERE WILL ALWAYS BE PAIN in the lives of people in organizations. We cannot prevent all of it, but organisations can create the conditions that keep many kinds of toxins at bay and maintain healthy workplaces.'

(Frost, 2003:185, emphasis original)

In writing this book, our aim has been to shine a light on the dark side of organisational life, particularly as it relates to emotional labour. We have attended to those tasks, relations and encounters that go unseen, that are talked about in private, that are often known only to those who belong to a given occupation. We have sought out those who are required to deal in aggression, either as the purveyors of antipathetic labour or as workers who must offer neutrality in the face of provocation. We have reflected on what it means to be associated with emotionally dirty work. We have also considered the consequences of the emotional pain that arises from the everyday functioning of organisations and that, if left untreated, can turn toxic. In short, we have sort to redress a trend that has seen these darker aspects of emotional labour underdeveloped and underresearched.

That is not to say that dealing in the dark side of emotional labour is always a negative experience. We have contemplated the ways in which dealing with the anxieties and despair of others is a considered a privilege by dirty workers (Chapter 4). We have noted the pride individuals take in using their understanding of and skills in emotional labour to manage the emotions of others through neutrality, de-escalation or empathetic care (Chapters 3 and 5). We have argued that the use of antipathetic emotional labour may be actively required in certain work roles and contexts pursuant to organisational goals (Chapter 2). We have also considered the ways in which emotional labour is both a source and a product of the emotional capital that individuals build over lifetimes (Chapter 6). In this sense emotional labour can speak to a capacity for certain types of work on the dark side of organisations – a valued and valuable asset to individual, organisation and society alike.

There are, then, positive aspects to the dark side of emotional labour that are difficult for outsiders to appreciate, not least because such facets tend to be written out of official organisational narratives and research accounts of rational practice. The dark side speaks to complex contexts for work in which emotional challenges, rewards and capacities are simultaneously eschewed and valued by individuals, organisations and society. By re-presenting such complexity we hope to encourage more managerial and academic interest in the dark side of emotional labour. Such interest would not, however, be complete without consideration of the responsibilities that arise from the effects of such work.

Emotional labour can take its toll on those who perform it when considered in sociological (e.g. symbolic, identity, care) and physiological (e.g. well-being, burnout, dissonance) terms. Symbolically, emotional dirty work can threaten to pollute the worker (Chapter 4) by dint of association with labours that suggest servility, lower social status or morally questionable actions (Kreiner *et al.*, 2006). Regardless of the self-worth and pride that workers may feel in undertaking emotional labour, contact with difficult emotions such as anger and despair can cause others to turn away for fear of being tainted themselves. Under such circumstances we can talk about certain types of emotional labour having identity consequences for workers as outsiders enquire, 'How could you do that?' (McMurray & Ward, 2014). Negative identity consequences can also arise from the type of emotional labour enacted. Take, for example, the emotional neutrality of the doctor's receptionist in the face of violence. Such neutrality can be read by the consumer as an absence of care and a failure to understand their individual plight. Such readings give way to characterisations of receptionists individually and collectively as 'dragons behind a desk' (Arber & Sawyer, 1985; McMurray & Ward, 2014). Such characterisations stand as a rebuttal to the occupational legitimacy and standing of receptionists. They speak to an attempt to undermine what is already an uncertain position of power. This uncertainty arises in part from the asymmetrical way in which feeling rules are applied to consumer and worker (see Chapter 3). In accordance with organisational feeling rules, workers must learn to control their darker feelings as part of a rationalised encounter with consumers (Warner, 2007), and yet those rules weigh heavily on workers (Sturdy & Fineman, 2001) insofar as emotional indiscretion on their part is more likely to be punished through employment sanction or job loss even as the customer, encouraged by the enchantment myth of consumer sovereignty, is indulged or even encouraged in abuse of the worker (Korczynski & Ott, 2004; Korczynski & Evans, 2013).

Then there is the toxicity (Chapter 5) that arises from the everyday pain of organising and that threatens to undermine the ability of individuals to do their jobs and, indeed, the effectiveness with which organisations execute their functions (Figley, 1995; Stein, 2007; Gabriel, 2012). We have seen how the effects of toxins can be mitigated by the work of toxin handlers who reframe painful encounters, facilitate sense making and offer care. While this work may be intrinsically satisfying for those who undertake it, such work tends to go underrewarded and underrecognised by formal organisational appraisal systems (Gallos, 2008). Indeed, there is evidence to suggest that handling toxins can harm your career as care of others means that your own allotted tasks go undone (Frost, 2003) and career aspirations falter.

While these effects speak to the sociological consequences of emotional labour as they relate to symbols, power, identity, change, action, conflict and meaning, the outcomes of such work may also be considered in physical and psychological terms. We saw in Chapter 2 how the use of aggression can be a source of adrenaline and pride (in the work of bouncers) but also a source of guilt as workers reflect on the effects of employing intimidation. In the work of police and prison officers, different forms of emotional intimidation may also speak to the imminent threat of physical peril and pain, such that emotional and physical harm are intertwined for labourers. Working with the difficult emotions of callers, patients and pet owners 'leaves a sticky mark' on labourers (Bergman & Chalkley, 2007) as key emotions and issues stay with them – even haunt them (McMurray & Ward, 2014). Then there are the well-rehearsed psychological concerns over burnout, emotional exhaustion, alienation, depersonalisation, stress, depression, miasma and self-estrangement that have been identified as potential consequences of emotional labour more generally (Hochschild, 1983; Ashforth & Humphrey, 1993; Ashforth & Tomiuk, 2000; Figley, 1995; Sturdy and Fineman, 2001; Frost, 2003; Gabriel, 2012). Such effects can render the worker cynical, insensitive and numb (Hochschild, 1983; Johnson, 2015).

Working on the dark side of emotional labour is, then, a complex process with widely varied outcomes: some positive, others negative. In this concluding chapter we want to consider what if any responsibility managers and employers might have for the effects of the dark side of emotional labour. While we acknowledge that an economic case may be made for attending to the effects of emotion labour (Frost, 2003), we want to argue the case for organisations adopting an *ethics of care* in respect of workers. Such an ethics implies treating workers as particular, special and deserving of our attention as ends in and of themselves, rather than as means to some other rational economic goal. We argue that such an ethics moves beyond the soft HR practices and rhetorics of care that are largely employed to garner subtly stronger control over workers. It moves beyond the tendency to 'talk' of care while simultaneously failing to reward and recognise such caring work. It eschews the rather cynical trend of espousing a concern for care all the while seeking to pass the resulting responsibility on to someone else – a trend Hochschild (2003:2) describes as a false ideology of care in which the practice and practicalities of caring have 'gone to hell'. Rather, in making the case for an ethics of care we seek to provide a theoretical foundation for practically supporting those who perform emotional labour. In order to do this, we move away from the witness accounts used thus far to consider some of the more conceptual justifications for employing an ethics of care in response to the emotional labours of workers. We consider what ethics means in organising and managing. We consider how ethics is often employed in a very limited rational sense to maintain existing priorities and how a different conception (based in what is described as a matrixial sensitivity, following Kenny & Fotaki, 2014) can better meet the needs of both organisations and workers. Having done so, we also consider the implications for managing, organising and caring, while acknowledging some of the challenges that remain when managers 'dare to care' (Phillips, 2015). We start by considering the limited ways in which 'ethics' is considered in many mainstream organisations at present, and why a rational economic 'ethics' is not enough to ensure that care is valued as an everyday practice.

Ethics and emotional labour

Given the potential costs and harms of emotional labour to the worker, it seems reasonable to enquire *where* responsibility for the well-being of emotional labourers lies. It can be argued that labourers, as paid workers, have some responsibility for their own choice of career and, as a consequence, for their individual well-being (though it might be noted that far from all of us choose where and at what we work). Accepting this, we might still argue that, given that employers profit from such labours, they may also have some responsibility for the emotional health of their workers in much the same way as they are responsible for physical safety. We might go as far as to enquire whether managers and employers have an *ethical* responsibility for the processes and effects of emotional labour on workers.

To speak of an 'ethical' responsibility is far from unproblematic when it comes to emotional labour insofar as dominant managerial approaches to ethics are said to revolve around a 'privileging of rationality, penchant for codification, tendency to self-congratulation, predilection to control, affinity to masculinity, blindness to justice, and subsumption under corporate goals' that are 'blind to affectual relations, care, compassion or any forms of feeling' (Pullen & Rhodes, 2014:1). Developing this line of analysis, Pullen and Rhodes (2014) argue that contemporary debates around organisational responsibilities and ethics are dominated by procedural concerns related to the desire to be seen as doing the right thing such as publishing ethical codes and practice protocols, all of which are predicated on maximising economic self-interest. The implication for emotional labourers is that attention to the processes of emotional labour and its effects on the worker will be considered only insofar as such action offers an economic benefit to the corporation itself (if it is considered at all, given the misguided undervaluing of emotional labour as women's work and apparently unskilled work).

Where such labour is recognised as a component in maximising economic returns, responsibility for the emotional well-being of workers is considered only when it sustains the effectiveness of service interactions and reduces the potential costs that result from labourers' stress, burnout, disengagement or outright resistance – costs that may manifest in absenteeism, turnover, misbehaviour and substance abuse (Sturdy & Fineman, 2001). Evidence for such costs – as revealed in conversations for this book – have included accounts of doctors' receptionists who struggle to maintain courteous and empathetic performance in the face of repeated abuse from patients, HR managers who have left posts due to emotional pain and toxicity, carers who have hit back at patients, and support workers who drink at home to cope with the effects of listening to other people's emotional pain. A chance conversation during the writing of this book offered a further example; it concerned a beauty therapist on an ocean cruise liner who used to lock herself in an equipment cupboard to escape the pressure of being continually on show emotionally (see also Tracy 2000). There is also the cabin crew who lock themselves in bedrooms and toilets just to be alone. These personal struggles become effectiveness issues when staff leave as a result or revolt, as in the case of the Jet Blue flight attendant who cursed out a difficult customer before exiting the plane via an emergency slide.

Each of these examples has the potential to impose costs on an organisation in terms of absenteeism, turnover, complaints, sabotage, bad publicity and reputational damage. Avoiding such costs is generally seen to mean controlling the long-term responses of the worker (Sturdy & Fineman, 2001). Such control is likely to include developing in workers the type of acting and detachment that speak to the highest standards of rational organising, while putting mechanisms in place to offer counselling and compassionate support when workers struggle to cope. Indeed, it has been suggested that experiencing compassion at work has the effect of increasing worker commitment to the organisation, which in turn reduces turnover and heightens the sense of working in a positive climate, while also aiding the recruitment of new staff who value such supportive environments (Madden *et al.*, 2012).

Considered in this way, caring for workers is reduced to calculating the advantage or opportunity costs of 'ethical behaviour'. Pullen and Rhodes (2014:2) argue that such calculation actually precludes the very possibility of ethical action because 'when organisations seek to define the interests of others in their own terms so that they can be controlled for the benefit of the corporation itself, then an ethics of genuine concern and respect for other people lies in tatters'. In essence, the only 'good' being considered is profit, with little concern for responsibility to others. We see what happens when ethical claims become little more than a pursuit of economic gains under another name in Johnson's (2015) study of Oakwood residential home. At Oakwood, managers were said to convince workers that it was their duty to perform emotional labour in the name of care, that they had a humanitarian obligation to gift their 'naturalised' emotional talents in the service of others in the same way that they might for their own family members. In this particular example, the imposition of such altruistic reasoning was said to have caused low-paid care workers to 'disregard their economic interests' (Johnson, 2015:123) as they campaigned for more resources for clients instead of better remuneration for their own material and immaterial labours. Moreover, it left workers open to emotional distress and harm as deep bonds of affection toward clients were severed by illness or death and workers were left bereft. In such cases rationality trumps emotion such that workers are controlled for the economic self-interests of a corporation that is seemingly content to externalise the costs to the individual of their emotional labours. The result is an 'ersatz morality' in which the employer promulgates the notion that workers have a vocational duty to give of themselves while labourers suspect that in reality corporations are 'just worried about the money' (Johnson, 2015:123). Under these conditions, talk of responsibilities and ethical duties has more to do with the efficient extraction of value from residents and workers on behalf of shareholders than with an ethics of care.

In such cases, talk of ethics in managing and organising is problematic because an 'ethics that privileges planning, predictability, control and measurement seems to forget the value of affectual relations, care, compassion or any other forms of feeling that are expressed' (Pullen & Rhodes, 2014:2); worse still, it may actively exploit affectual relations in pursuit of personal gain. If anything, such cases speak of an *ethics of violence* (McMurray, 2015) in which the interests of one party (the employer) are promoted over those of another (emotional labourers) in the name of caring for a third (resident customers). Where a concern for self overrides a concern for other and where reason pushes out emotion, it appears that talk of ethics is rendered meaningless and an ethical claim to care for emotional labours remains unrecognised.

To reiterate, emotional labour is an increasingly crucial if often under-recognised and underremunerated part of organising and work. Lack of recognition has often led to a lack of support for those carrying out such work. While emotional labourers may evince a sense of pride in maintaining their own coping strategies individually or collectively (e.g. through informal sense making or depersonalising encounters), it remains apposite to enquire whether such self-sufficiency absolves employers and managers of their responsibility to care. A rational case can be made for offering support in terms of reducing the turnover, absenteeism and service failures that are associated with the dysfunctional effects of emotional labour. Such justification speaks to a rational interest in the self over and above any (ethical) concern for those who perform such work. Moreover, under such conditions support for workers will be offered and maintained only as long as it is shown to be efficient or profitable. We suggest that responsibility for the effects of emotional labour can and should mean something more. Specifically, a consideration of ethics requires that 'other' (rather than self) be placed at the centre of our concerns as part of a commitment to care. It is our contention that to require someone to employ emotional labour is to place ourselves as manager/employer/colleague/customer in a position of responsibility regarding the effect of those labours – it opens organisational actors up to claims of a duty of care and requires the adoption of an ethics of care.

Emotional labour and an ethics of care

Gabriel (2009) states that, rather than seeking to establish universal principles, an 'ethics of care' is concerned with how people might 'sustain fragile networks of relations that allow people to grow and prosper, developing trust, respect and responsibility to each other' (Gabriel, 2009:383). For Gabriel this implies treating people under your care as special and attending to them as individuals for whom special provisions and allowances are to be made.

Arising out of feminist theories of business ethics (Derry, 2002), an ethics of care places greater priority on relationships, nurturing and praxis than do mainstream/malestream theories that prioritise principles, justice, rights and individual autonomy. It is an approach to ethics that requires attention to the specificities of the person in front of us, rather than adherence to predetermined principles that we stand behind. It also acknowledges that ethical concerns are also intimately political in nature (Phillips, 2015) insofar as attending to ethics requires critique of established practices, norms, values, resource allocations and power structures (Derry, 2002; Pullen & Rhodes, 2015). This, in turn, suggests a repositioning of how we see the relationship between work and life.

Reconnecting work with life

An ethics of care challenges the presumption that managing, organising and business are in some way disconnected from and outside the rest of life. It challenges us to see work, managing and organising as part of wider processes of living and, in so doing, recognises that emotions, embodiment, truth, beauty, compassion and care have value in their own rights alongside reason, efficiency and profit (Rynes *et al.*, 2012). Indeed, for some commentators, care and compassion are defining elements of what it means to be human – part of an innate ability to forgo self-interest to attend to the needs and suffering of others (Madden *et al.*, 2012). Considered thus, to talk about care is not to introduce something new into collective life but rather to reintroduce that which has been erroneously pushed out by the march of rationality.

An ethics of care is particularly well suited to organising contexts insofar as it speaks to the need for action. As we consider later, it is based in and focuses on the tangible issues that confront us, rather than the creation and application of abstract sets of principles. It challenges us to see our interconnectedness as organisational actors and to 'dare to care' about those connections in practice (Phillips, 2015). An ethics of care is linked to action and decision wherein those offering care face the choice of supporting the other or else withdrawing, ignoring or harming. Where the decision is taken to care, Phillips (2015:59) suggests that it involves those practices that

> maintain, promote or enhance the flourishing and well-being of relevant parties and which recognise that flourishing of the particular is connected to the flourishing of the general and vice versa.
>
> (Phillips, 2015:59)

Theoretical support for such a position is also offered by Kenny and Fotaki's (2014) account of matrixial border spaces and ethics. In a paper that seeks to move beyond established dichotomies of reason and emotion, masculine and feminine, 'other' and 'I', Kenny and Fotaki (2014) make the case for focusing on the spaces, networks and connections that bind organisational actors (rather than on the differences that separate them). Drawing on the work of Bracha Ettinger, Kenny and Fotaki (2014) argue for a matrixial conception of ethics that employs the metaphor of the womb to speak to the separate yet intimately connected lives of mother and unborn child – two individuals defined by an interdependent relationship. Kenny and Fotaki (2014:2) argue that a matrixial conceptualisation of ethics based on the ideas of necessary connectivity, inclusivity and compassion can be used to emphasise the importance of cohabitation and joint relational spaces between different individuals. When applied to organisational contexts, such a perspective acknowledges the essential differences that exist among people while at the same time speaking to relations of dependence that not only bind us but also implicate us in the necessary care of one another.

These connections and interdependencies are endlessly enacted and reproduced at a local level in the relations of worker and manager, buyer and seller, manufacturer and supplier, customer and retailer, creditor and debtor, student and teacher, trainer and apprentice, patient and nurse, venture capitalist and business, micro-entrepreneur and crowd funder, emotional labourer and customer (to name but a few). These connections multiply until the need to consider dependence and compassion are writ on a massive scale with global financial crises, global terrorism, global climate change, global supply chains and global poverty all speaking to the ways in which we are connected to multiple others. Rynes *et al.* (2012:504) make the point as follows:

> As organisations, nations, and people become more interdependent, collaboration and coordination become more essential to the achievement of both individual and collective goals. Care and compassion, which are grounded in relationships and relatedness, have much to contribute to an interconnected, suffering, and surprising world.

A matrixial sensitivity acknowledges the relations of dependence that not only bind us but also implicate us in the necessary care of one another, while not seeking to erase or ignore the essential differences that exist between us. It suggests a modified form of organic solidarity (in a Durkheimian sense) where the individualism of industrial and postindustrial societies is increasingly tempered by growing appreciation of the complexity of our interdependence economically, materially, intellectually and socially such that it is both desirable and necessary to care about the well-being of others (Rynes *et al.*, 2012). Just as important, a matrixial sensitivity promises to allow ethics back into organising so as to balance the claims of reason, efficiency and profit. It allows us to recognise that self-interest is not the only driver of human action (Rynes *et al.*, 2012). As such, the case for caring for emotional labourers no longer depends solely on instrumental and economic reasoning but may be pursued in light of our acknowledged dependence and relationality such that we 'dare to care' (Phillips, 2015) for the other. It effectively challenges 'the low value placed on caring' which, as Hochschild notes, 'results neither from an absence of a need for it nor from the simplicity or ease of doing it. Rather . . . from a cultural politics of inequality' (Hochschild, 2003:196).

Fragilised rather than paternalistic care

By recognising that who we are and what we achieve in organisational contexts is intimately dependent on our relations with others, a matrixial sensitivity opens us up to the need to care for others. A matrixial approach to caring is not, however, the same as that to be found in paternalistic approaches. Specifically, the former does not claim to fully know the 'other' to whom care is being offered and does not presume that the other is simply another of me (Rhodes, 2012). It does not therefore prescribe strict adherence to a set of universal principles or rules that are handed down from on high (Gabriel 2009; Phillips, 2015). While an ethics of care may be informed by concerns for justice and guided by general values, its worth lies in the practice of a situated universalism such that broad responsibilities are understood and enacted in response to the specificities of particular people's lives (Phillips, 2015). Acceptance of the unknowability of the other means that a presumption to understand what is best for that other cannot rationally be sustained. In place of the presumption to 'know' workers (and thus impose universal prescriptions), Kenny and Fotaki (2014:10) speak to an encounter based on 'fascination and awe' in which the other is seen as connected to yet different from the self. They challenge the 'neoliberal project that assumes the existence of an impermeable individualised subject, by bringing in the idea of human connectivity and injuriousness' such that the subject/worker/manager is established as a 'relational and interdependent being' (Kenny & Fotaki, 2014:10).

Reference to injuriousness reminds us of our shared fragility arising from our corporeal forms and our communally embodied spaces that speak to a range of senses and experiences beyond reason but without denying reason. When linked to an ethics of care it has the value of 'recognizing vulnerability as ubiquitous, and valuing growth in the cared-for and uncertain future' (Rynes *et al.*, 2012:514). We have seen that emotional labour is inherently uncertain insofar is it can be a source of pride and pain – the work of Samaritans being a case in point (Chapters 4 and 5; McMurray & Ward, 2014). Moreover, such uncertainty is encountered differently across different workers and indeed by the same worker over time. It is also a practice that is clearly embodied insofar as emotional displays require manipulation and presentation of the worker's body through uniforms, smiles and assertive postures, while its effects are also written on the body in terms of tension, stress, physical harm and exhilaration. A matrixial response to such individual encounters suggests a process of opening up or 'self-fragilisation' such that 'the experience of becoming open, "fragile" and therefore vulnerable, is central to enabling an encounter with the other that does not attempt to dominate and oppress them, as otherwise might occur' but instead 'opening up the self generously towards the other' (Kenny & Fotaki, 2014:7). This means support is not forced upon emotional labours where it is not required, but where a need is announced, support is offered in a way that responds to the individual's needs (rather than proffering off-the-shelf solutions and top-down principles). Responding to specific needs requires paying attention to the specificities of the other's emotional labour and life, rather than offering solutions based wholly on our own experiences. This begins by being open to the other and treating her individual experiences and needs as important. It implies making space for care.

Space for an ethics of care

An ethics of care informed by a matrixial sensitivity requires that a sense of cherishing others be reintroduced into everyday organising, including sites of emotional labour. Put another way, it is about an ethics that develops 'caring-for as nonabusive and nonexploitative such that a relational sense of self and willingness to embrace the difference of the other and to care for them includes contexts outside those already established as appropriate arenas for caring' (Phillips, 2015:60). Such an ethics sounds idealistic only where care has been driven out of contemporary modes of organising. Where rationalisation has been taken to imply the intensified march of efficiency and economy to the exclusion of all else, then, yes, to talk of care seems utopian. And yet we have seen that emotional labourers and toxin handlers readily offer care to those with whom they work. Whether it be taking on the emotional pain of peers, making sense of the frustration of clients, or working to offer compassion or joy to customers through acts that go well beyond formal task descriptions and informal feeling rules, everyday organising is replete with care.

Why do these everyday practices of care matter? For Frost (2003:186) they matter because recognising what people think and feel 'affects, for better or worse, the emotional tone and level of toxicity in the workplace'. It is for this reason that Frost argues for the development of organisational cultures in which individuals 'feel equitably acknowledged, celebrated and compensated for their work' (Frost, 2003:190). While the emphasis on equity edges toward the type of 'ethics of justice' that Gabriel (2009) rejects on the basis that it treats all as formally equal and subject to general principles, Frost's position does nonetheless encourage organisations to attend to individual needs through listening and training and by offering a chance to learn from difficulties and mistakes rather than suffering punishment. Frost (2003) acknowledges that bolt-on systems or principles for dealing with emotional pain and toxicity are unlikely to be effective if they are not matched by an organisational culture and ethos that fundamentally values people (a point highlighted in Johnson's [2015] study of Oakwood care home). Indeed, a failure to keep social, psychological and emotional contracts with workers is likely to be counterproductive as workers respond negatively to perceived betrayals (Frost, 2003). That said, managers and leaders can have a crucial role in facilitating such cultures insofar as the authority and resources invested in their hierarchical position increase their relative ability to shape the work environment. Specifically, managers and leaders have relatively greater power to influence those behaviours that are rewarded and punished, the nature and extent of training, responses to emotional labour and its effects, support for toxin handlers and the provision of space for individual needs.

We are not saying that responsibility for an ethics of care resides solely with managers and leaders. To do so is tantamount to encouraging the top-down paternalism that a matrixially informed ethics of care serves to critique. Care and compassion can and do arise as spontaneous acts between colleagues (Madden *et al.*, 2012). This is most evident at times of personal or collective crises (e.g. the death of a colleague, the response to the 9/11 or 7/7 attacks). Under these circumstances compassion is said to reflect an innate human response to another's suffering, anguish or pain, wherein we forgo self-interest in the care of others (Madden *et al.*, 2012). Such spontaneous compassion reminds us that all members of an organisation contribute to its cultures, practices and orders (Strauss, 1978) and that peers can assist in the management of emotional labour. To this end, Samaritans break from taking phone calls to work through the difficult emotions that follow the empathetic treatment of a suicide call; door staff recount and compare experiences of aggression when dealing with drunk and unruly punters; veterinary staff make sense of the upset and anger of pet owners by telling each other that such anger is a consequence of the latter's grief and guilt; and prison officers step in for one another when it becomes clear that the other is struggling to maintain a neutral performance in the face of provocation – effectively recognising and responding to the person's observed organisational pain.

These types of bottom-up responses to pain and toxicity are generally offered in addition to individuals' organisationally prescribed roles and responsibilities (Frost, 2003). Where this extra care is widespread, it may inform the culture of the organisation, increasing the extent to which it is perceived to be compassionate and responsive (Madden *et al.*, 2012). Managers and leaders can seek to develop such cultures by allowing space for informal support. For example, the tendency for Samaritans to stop their work in order to support a colleague struggling with the effects of emotional labour is supported, recognised and encouraged by organisational policy and practice that decree that such a response is acceptable and, indeed, a recognised part of each worker's role. Samaritans abide by this policy and practice because they understand that they cannot provide emotional support to clients if the workers are not in a good emotional position themselves. Care of self and colleagues is therefore recognised as an essential prerequisite for effective emotional labour. The approach taken to peer-to-peer care by Samaritans is possible only when organisations make space for compassionate responses to the pain of others. Where work is rationalised and intensified to the utmost degree, the space for care is removed.

A matrixially informed ethics of care opens up the possibility of valuing emotional labours and the people who perform such labour as ends in and of themselves. It provides a basis for offering care that goes beyond a simple rational economic case without necessarily refuting the latter. Of course there are costs associated with offering care. First, there is a danger that the offer care will be abused (Phillips, 2015), that space for coping will be used for soldiering or avoidance of legitimate work. To this we might add the danger of harming the interests of one party while caring for the interests of another party. For example, protecting employees from harm may require refusing to serve abusive customers, thus destroying the myth of consumer sovereignty and risking the latter's wrath through online reviews that affect the reputation and success of the business. Finally, there is the danger that caring will continue to be marginalised as a feminine activity and as such remain undervalued and underrewarded. Under such conditions 'caring' can be used to reinforce the separation of rational/masculine/ skilled/valued practices on the one hand from emotional/feminine/natural/ undervalued practices on the other. Following Kenny and Fotaki (2014), we urge the rejection of such dichotomies. We do not believe that it is fruitful to pursue such distinctions; moreover, they do not resonate with our experiences of organisational life. Emotions are an increasingly integral part of service economies and work. These contexts require the deployment of what are traditionally seen as masculine (antipathetic) and feminine (empathetic) performances by men and women according to the particularities of context (the work of male and female bouncers being a case in point). We also reject the suggestion that emotional labour is unskilled. Indeed, we have argued that the ability to effectively empathise, perform neutrality or evoke antipathy draws on the emotional capital accrued by labourers over a lifetime (see Chapter 6). Such skills are often honed and required by employing organisations. Is it not therefore time for the value of such work to be appropriately recognised in the reward and support systems that are offered at work?

Living the dark side of emotional labour

In drawing this book to a close we have sought to make a case for the adoption of an ethics of care in respect of emotional labour. We have done so not because emotional labour is always and necessarily harmful or because those who undertake such work are incapable of taking care of themselves. We hope to have shown through the experiences of volunteers, police officers, bankers, lawyers, veterinarians, carers, bouncers and others that working on the dark side of emotional labour can be a rewarding and positive experience in which individuals can take pride. We have also offered accounts of the sense making, reframing, refocusing, depersonalising and capital that are employed as part of individual and collective processes of coping. We talk, then, of the dark side of emotional labour not because it is essentially negative but rather because it is all too often unseen, underrecognised and undervalued. Like the dark side of the moon, it speaks to a place that most of us cannot see, will not visit and may struggle to understand. One of the intentions of this book has been to shed light on this unfamiliar surface and in so doing begin to reveal some of its rich and complex variation. It is rich in terms of the multiplicity of occupations, tasks, opportunities and challenges to which it speaks in organising terms. It is complex insofar as it describes a context for organising in which rationality and emotions sit side by side and where the use of negative emotions can have positive effects, while displays of empathy come at cost (or not, as the case may be).

It is concern with the potential costs – in their widest sense – of emotional labour that brought us to a consideration of ethics and care. Our aim has been to make a case and a space for an ethics of care in its own right. Yes, there are good economic reasons to guard against dissonance, burnout, turnover, absenteeism and resistance as a consequence of emotional labour, but there is also an ethical claim to be made for offering care on its own terms, because we recognise people as human beings with feelings, because we value our connections to others and because we feel a sense of personal responsibility in the face of the other – in the face of those who work for our benefit on the dark side of emotional labour. Is it possible that an ethics of care can stand as a decent response to the lament of the police officer at the beginning of this book?

'You created my job, you created me. To you, I am a robot in uniform. You press the button and when you call me to the scene you expect results. But I'm also a man. I even have a heart.' Vincent Maher, Policeman

(Terkel, 1974:137)

An ethics of care takes time; it requires an opening up of self individually and organisationally and empathy in the face of others. That it can be a difficult voluntary process that aims for the care of others, rather than seeking to benefit oneself, is what marks it as an ethical undertaking. It requires that we care for the managed heart.

References

Abraham, R. (1998) Emotional dissonance in organizations: Antecedents, consequences, and moderators. *Genetic Social and General Psychology Monographs*, 124: 229–246.

Abraham, R. (1999) The impact of emotional dissonance on organizational commitment and intention to turnover. *The Journal of Psychology*, 133: 441–455.

Abraham, R. (2000) The role of job control as a moderator of emotional dissonance and emotional intelligence-outcome relationships. *The Journal of Psychology*, 134: 169–184.

Ackroyd, S., & Crowdy, P. (1990) Can culture be managed? Working with 'raw' material: the case of English Slaughtermen. *Personnel Review* 19 (5): 3–13.

Ackroyd, S., & Thompson, P. (1999) *Organizational Misbehaviour*. London: Sage.

Allatt, P. (1993) Becoming privileged: the role of family processes. In I. Bates and G. Riseborough (eds), *Youth and inequality*. Buckingham: Open University Press.

Alvesson, M., & Willmott, H. (2002) Identity regulation as organizational control: producing the appropriate individual. *Journal of Management Studies* 39(5): 619–644.

Arber, S., & Sawyer, L. (1985) The roll of the receptionist in general practice: A 'dragon behind a desk'? *Social Science & Medicine* 20(9): 911–921.

Ashforth, R., & Humphrey, B. (1993) Emotional labour in service roles: The influence of identity. *The Academy of Management Review* 18(1): 88–118.

Ashforth, B., & Kreiner, G. (1999) 'How can you do it?': Dirty work and the challenge of constructing a positive identity. *Academy of Management Review* 24(3): 413–434.

Ashforth, B., Kreiner, G., Clark, M., & Fugate, M. (2007) Normalizing dirty work: Managerial tactics for countering occupational taint. *Academy of Management Journal* 50(1): 149–174.

Ashforth, B. E., & Tomuik, M. A. (2000) Emotional labour and authenticity: Views from service agents. In S. Fineman (ed.), *Emotions in Organizations* (2nd ed.). London: Sage.

Ashforth, B. E., & Kreiner, G. E. (2002) Normalizing emotion in organizations: Making the extraordinary seem ordinary. *Human Resource Management Review* 12(2): 215–235.

Atkinson, P. (1995) *Medical Talk and Medical Work*. London: Sage.

Banerjee, S. B., & Linstead, S. A. (2001) Globalization, multiculturalism and other fictions: The new colonization for the new millennium. *Organization* 8: 711–750.

Barger, P. B., & Grandey, A. A. (2006) "Service with a smile and encounter satisfaction" : Emotional contagion and appraisal mechanisms. *Academy of Management Journal* 49(6): 1229–1238.

Barker, J. (1993) Tightening the iron cage: Concertive control in self-managed teams. *Administrative Science Quarterly* 38: 408–437.

Barsade, S. (2002) The ripple effect: Emotional contagion in groups. *Administrative Science Quarterly* 47(4): 644–675.

Bates, I. (1991) Closely observed training: An exploration of links between social structures, training and identity. *International Studies in Sociology of Education* 1: 225–243.

Bergman, M., & Chalkley, K. (2007) 'Ex' marks a spot: The stickiness of dirty work and other removed stigmas. *Journal of Occupational Health Psychology* 12(3): 251–265.

Bolton, S.C. (2000) Who cares? Offering emotion work as a 'gift' in the nursing labour process. *Journal of Advanced Nursing* 32(3): 580–586.

Bolton, S.C. (2005) Women's work, dirty work: The gynaecology nurse as 'other'. *Gender, Work & Organization* 12(2): 169–186.

Bolton, S.C. (2009) Getting to the heart of the emotional labour process: A reply to Brook. *Work, Employment and Society* 23(3): 549–560.

Bolton, S.C. (2010) Old ambiguities and new developments: Exploring the emotional labour process. In P. Thompson and C. Smith (eds), *Working Life: Renewing Labour Process Analysis*. London: Palgrave Macmillan.

Borysensko, J. (1988) *Minding the Body, Mending the Mind*. New York: Bantam.

Bourdieu, P. (1977) *Outline of a Theory of Practice*. Cambridge: Cambridge University Press.

Bourdieu, P. (1986) *Distinction: A Social Critique of the Judgement of Taste*. London: Routledge.

Bourdieu, P. (1989) Social space and symbolic power. *Sociological Theory* 7: 14–25.

Bourdieu, P. (1990) *The Logic of Practice*. Cambridge: Polity Press.

Braverman, H. (1974) *Labour and Monopoly Capital: The Degradation of Work in the Twentieth Century*. London: Monthly Review Press.

Brook, P. (2007) Customer orientated militants? A critique of the customer orientated bureaucracy theory on front-line service worker collectivism. *Work Employment & Society* 21(2): 363–374.

Brook, P. (2009) In critical defence of emotional labour: Refuting Bolton's critique of Hochschild's concept. *Work, Employment & Society* 23(3): 531–548.

Bunting, M. (2004) *Willing Slaves*. London: Harper Collins.

Cahill, S. (1999) Emotional capital and professional socialisation: The case of mortuary science students (and me). *Social Psychology Quarterly* 62: 101–116.

Callahan, J.L., & McCollum, E.E. (2002) Obscured variability: The distinction between emotion work and emotional labour. In N. Ashkanasy, W. J. Zerbe and C. Hartel (eds), *Managing Emotions in the Workplace*. New York: M. E. Sharpe.

Campbell, A. (2000) *The Scottish Miners 1874–1939. Vol. 1: Industry, Work and Community*. Aldershot: Ashgate.

Carey, M. (2014) Mind the gaps: Understanding the rise and implications of different types of cynicism within statutory social work. *British Journal of Social Work* 44(1): 127–144.

Chiappetta-Swanson, C. (2005) Dignity and dirty work: Nurses' experiences in managing genetic termination for foetal anomaly. *Qualitative Sociology* 28(1): 93–115.

Clegg, S., & Baumeler, C. (2010) Essay: From iron cages to liquid modernity in organizational analysis. *Organization Studies* 3112): 1713–1733.

Colley, H., James, D., Diment, K., & Tedder, M. (2007) Learning as becoming in vocational education and training: Class, gender and the role of vocational habitus. *Journal of Vociational Education & Training* 55(4): 471–497.

Collinson, D., & Hearn, J. (1996) *Men as Managers, Managers as Men*. London: Sage.

Collinson, M., & Collinson, D. (1996) 'It's only dick': The sexual harassment of women managers in insurance sales. *Work, Employment & Society* 10(1): 29–56.

Connell, R. W. (2000) *The Men and the Boys*. Oxon: Allen & Unwin.

Derry, R. (2002) Feminist theory and business ethics. In R. Frederick (ed.), *A Companion to Business Ethics*. Oxford: Blackwell.

Dickens, C. (1857/1996) *Little Dorrit*. London: Wordsworth Classics.

Diefendorff, J. M., Richard, E. M., & Croyle, M. H. (2006) Are emotional display rules formal job requirements? Examination of employee and supervisor perceptions. *Journal of Occupational and Organizational Psychology* 79: 273–298.

Donkin, R. (2001) *Blood, Sweat and Tears: The Evolution of Work*. London: Texere.

Douglas, M. (1966) *Purity and Danger: An Analysis of Concepts of Pollution and Taboo*. London: Routledge.

Ekman, P. (1973) Cross culture studies of facial expressions. In P. Ekman (ed.), *Darwin and Facial Expressions: A Century of Research in Review*. New York: Academic Press.

Erickson, R. J., & Ritter, C. (2001) Emotional labour, burnout and inauthenticity: Does gender matter? *Social Psychology Quarterly* 64(2): 146–163.

Figley, C. R. (1995) *Compassion Fatigue: Coping with Secondary Traumatic Stress Disorder in Those That Treat the Traumatized*. New York: Brunner-Mazel.

Fineman, S. (1999) Emotion and organising. In S. Clegg and C. Hardy (eds), *Studying Organization: Theory and Method*. London: Sage.

Fineman, S. (2001) *Emotions in Organizations*. London: Sage.

Fleming, P. (2013) 'Down with Big Brother! The end of 'corporate culturalism'? *Journal of Management Studies* 50: 474–495.

Foucault, M. (1977/1991) *Discipline and Punish: The Birth of the Prison*. London: Penguin.

Freire, P. (1992) *Pedagogy of the Oppressed*. Harmondsworth: Penguin.

Frost, P. (2003) *Toxic Emotions at Work*. Boston: Harvard Business School Press.

Frost, P., & Robinson, S. (1999) The toxic handler: Organizational hero and casualty. *Harvard Business Review* 77: 96–106.

Gabriel, Y. (2009) Reconciling an ethic of care with Critical Management Pedagogy. *Management Learning* 40(4): 379–385.

Gabriel, Y. (2012) Organizations in a state of darkness: Towards a theory of organizational miasma. *Organization Studies* 33(9): 1137–1152.

Gallos, J. (2008) Learning from the toxic trenches: The winding road to healthier organizations – and to healthy everyday leaders. *Journal of Management Inquiry* 17(4): 354–367.

Gillies, V. (2006) Working class mothers and school life: Exploring the role of emotional capital. *Gender and Education* 18(3): 281–293.

Goffman, E. (1959) *The Presentation of Self in Everyday Life*. London: Penguin.

Goffman, E. (1997) The Stigmatized Self. In C. Lemert and A. Branaman (eds), *The Goffman Reader*. London: Blackwell.

Goleman, D. (1995) *Emotional Intelligence*. New York: Bantam.

Goleman, D. (1996) Emotional intelligence: why it can matter more than IQ. London: Bloomsbury.

Goudreau, J. (2013) From crying to temper tantrums: How to manage emotions at work. Forbes online. www.forbes.com/sites/jennagoudreau/2013/01/09/from-crying-to-temper-tantrums-how-to-manage-emotions-at-work/ (accessed 27/1/2015).

Grandey, A. (2008) Emotions at work: A review and research agenda. In C. Cooper and J. Barling (eds), The *SAGE Handbook of Organizational Behavior*. Thousand Oaks, CA: Sage.

Gray, C. (2009) *A Very Short, Fairly Interesting and Reasonably Cheap Book about Studying Organizations*. London: Sage.

Griffin, R.W., & O'Leary-Kelly, A. M. (2004) *The Dark Side of Organizational Behaviour*. San Francisco: Jossey-Bass.

Guy, M. E., & Newman, M. A. (2004) Women's jobs, men's jobs: Sex segregation and emotional labour. *Public Administration Review* 64(3): 289–298.

Guardian, The (2011) JetBlue flight attendant Steven Slater sentenced to 1 years' probation. www.theguardian.com/world/2011/oct/20/steven-slater-jetblue-flight-attendant-sentence (accessed 23/2/2015).

Guerrier, Y., & Adbi, A. (2003) Work at leisure and leisure at work: A study of the emotional labour of tour reps. *Human Relations* 56(11): 1399–1417.

Haber, D., Roby, J., & High-George, L. (2011) Stigma by association: The effects of caring for HIV/AIDS patients in South Africa. *Health & Social Care in the Community* 19(5): 541–549.

Hancock, P., & Tyler, M. (2001) *Work, Postmodernism and Organization: A Critical Introduction*. London: Sage.

Harker, R., Mahar, C., & Wilkes, C. (eds) *An Introduction to the Work of Pierre Bourdieu: The Practice of Theory*. London: Macmillan.

Harlow, E., Hearn, J., & Parkin W. (1995) Gendered noise: Organisations and the silence and din of domination. In C. Itzen and J. Newman (eds), *Gender Culture and Organizational Change: Putting Theory into Practice*. London: Routledge.

Hatfield, E., Cacioppo, J., & Rapson, R. L. (2004) *Emotional Contagion*. New York: Cambridge University Press.

Hayward, R.M., & Tuckey, M.R. (2011) Emotions in uniform: How nurses regulate emotion at work via emotional boundaries. *Human Relations* 64(11): 1501–1523.

Hobbs, D., Hadfield, P., Lister, S., & Winlow, S. (2002) 'Door Lore': The art and economics of intimidation. *British Journal of Criminology*, 42: 352–370.

Hochschild, A. (1983) *The Managed Heart: Commercialization of Human Feeling*. Berkeley: University of California Press.

Hochschild, A. (2003) *The Commercialization of Intimate Life: Notes from Home and Work*. Berkeley: University of California Press.

Hochschild, A.R. (1975) The sociology of feeling and emotion: Selected possibilities. In A. Millman and R. Moss Kanter (eds), *Another Voice*. New York: Anchor.

Hochschild, A. R. (1979) Emotion work, feeling rules and social structure. *American Journal of Sociology*: 551–575.

Hochschild, A.R. (1989) Reply to Cas Wouter's review essay on The Managed Heart. *Theory, Culture and Society* 6: 439–445.

Hochschild, A. R. (2003) *The Second Shift*. London: Penguin.

Holman, D., Martinez-Inigo, D., & Totterdell, P. (2008) Emotional labour and employee well-being an integrative view. In N. Ashkanasy and C. L. Cooper (eds), *Research Companion to Emotions in Organisations*. Cheltenham: Edward-Elgar.

Huffington Post (2012) www.huffingtonpost.com/2012/06/29/jose-serrano-american-eag_n_1636912.html (accessed 15/7/2015).

Hughes, E. (1951) Studying the nurse's work. *The American Journal of Nursing* 51(5): 294–295.

Hughes, E. (1958) *Men and Their Work*. Glencoe, IL: The Free Press.

Hughes, E. (1962) Good people and dirty work. *Social Problems* 10(1): 3–11.

Hughes, E. (1984) *The Sociological Eye*. New York: Transaction.

Humphrey, R. H. (2013) How leading with emotional labour creates common identities. In M. Iszatt-White (ed.), *Leadership as Emotional Labour*. Oxford: Routledge.

Humphrey, R. H., Pollack, J. M., & Hawver, T. H. (2008) Leading with emotional labour. *Journal of Managerial Psychology* 23: 151–168.

Illouz, E. (1997) 'Who will care for the caretaker's daughter?': Towards a sociology of happiness in the era of reflexive modernity. *Theory, Culture & Society* 14(4): 31–66.

James, N. (1989) Emotional labour: Skill and work in the social regulation of feelings. *Sociological Review* 37: 15–42.

James, N. (1992) Care = organization + physical labour + emotional labour. *Sociology of Health and Illness* 14(4): 488–509.

Jervis, L. (2001) The pollution of incontinence and the dirty work of caregiving in a US nursing home. *Medical Anthropology Quarterly* 15(1): 84–99.

Johnson, E. (2015) The business of care: The moral labour of care workers. *Sociology of Health and Illness* 37(1): 112–126.

Kenny, K., & Fotaki, M. (2014) From gendered organizations to compassionate borderspaces: Reading corporeal ethics with Bracha Ettinger. *Organization* 22(2): 183–199.

Klein, N. (2007) *The Shock Doctrine: The Rise of Disaster Capitalism*. New York: Metropolitan.

Korczynski, M. (2001) The contraditions in service work: Call centre as customer-oriented bureaucracy. In A. Sturdy, I. Grugulis and H. Willmott (eds), *Customer Service: Empowerment and Entrapment* (Critical Perspectives on Work and Organisations). London: Palgrave.

Korczynski, M. (2002) *Human Resource Management in Service Work*. Basingstoke: Palgrave.

Korczynski, M. (2003) Communities of coping: Collective emotional labour in service work. *Organization* 10(1): 55–79.

Korczynski, M., & Evans, C. (2013) Customer abuse to service workers: An analysis of its social creation within the service economy. *Work Employment & Society* 27(5): 768–784.

Korczynski, M., & Ott, U. (2004) When production and consumption meet: Cultural contradictions and the enchanting myth of consumer sovereignty. *Journal of Management Studies* 41: 575–599.

Kreiner, G., Ashforth, B., & Sluss, D. (2006) Identity dynamics in occupational dirty work: Integrating social identity and system justification perspectives. *Organization Science* 17(5): 619–636.

Leidner, R. (1993) *Fast Food Fast Talk: Service Work and the Routinization of Everyday Life*. Berkeley: University of California Press.

Letiche, H. (2009) Reflexivity and affectivity. *Culture and Organization* 15(3–4): 291–306.

Linstead, S. L., Marechal, G., & Griffin, R. W. (2010) The dark side of organization. *Organization Studies* 31(8): 1170–1172.

Linstead, S. L., Marechal, G., & Griffin, R. W. (2014) Theorizing the dark side of organizations. *Organization Studies* 35(2): 165–188.

Lively, K. J. (2002) Client contact and emotional labour: Upsetting the balance and evening the field. *Work and Occupations* 29(2): 198–225.

Loader, I. (2000) Plural policing and democratic governance. *Social and Legal Studies* 9(3): 323–346.

Lopez, S. H. (2006) Emotional labour and organized emotional care: Conceptualising nursing home care work. *Work & Occupations* 33(2): 133–160.

Madden, L., Duchon, D., Madden, T., & Plowman, D. (2012) Emergent organizational capacity for compassion. *Academy of Management Review* 37(4): 689–708.

Manion, C. (2007) Feeling, thinking, doing: Emotional capital, empowerment and women's education. In I. Epstein (ed.), *Recapturing the Personal: Essays on Education and Embodied Knowledge in Comparative Perspective*. Charlotte: Information Age.

McCabe, D. (2014) Light in the darkness? Managers in the back office of a Kafkaesque bank. *Organization Studies* 35: 255–278.

McClure, R., & Murphy, C. (2008) Contesting the dominance of emotional labour in professional nursing. *Journal of Health Organization and Management* 21(2): 101–120.

McIvor, A. (2013) *Working Lives: Work in Britain since 1945*. Palgrave: London.

McMurray, R. (2012) Embracing dirt in nursing matters, In R. Simpson, N, Slutskaya, P. Lewis and H. Hopfl (eds), *Dirty Work Concepts and Identities*. Basingstoke: Palgrave Macmillan.

McMurray, R. (2015) Care as politics: Ethics as violence. In A. Pullen and C. Rhodes (eds), *The Routledge Companion to Ethics, Politics and Organizations*. London: Routledge.

McMurray, R., Pullen, A., & Rhodes, C. (2011) Ethical subjectivity and politics in organizations: A case of health care tendering. *Organization* 18(4): 541–561.

McMurray, R., & Ward, J. (2014) 'Why would you want to do that?' Defining emotional dirty work. *Human Relations* 67(9): 1123–1143.

Meara, H. (1974) Honor in dirty work: The case of American meat cutters and Turkish butchers, *Sociology of Work and Occupations* 1(3): 259–283.

Mesmer-Magnus, J. R., DeChurch, L. A., & Wax, A. (2012) Moving emotional labour beyond surface and deep acting: A discordance-congruence perspective. *Organisational Psychology Review* 2(1): 6–53.

Mestrovic, S. G. (1997) *Postemotional Society*. London: Sage.

Mills, M., Drew, S., & Gassaway, B. (2007). Concluding thoughts. In S. Drew, M. Mills and B. Gassaway (eds), *Dirty Work*, Texas: Baylor University Press.

Morris, J. A., & Feldman, D. C. (1996) The dimensions, antecedents and consequences of emotional labour. *Academy of Management Review* 21(4): 986–1010.

Muhr, S. L., & Rehn, A. (2014) Branding atrocity: Narrating dark sides and managing organizational image. *Organization Studies* 35: 209–231.

Mullen, K. (1993) *A Healthy Balance: Glaswegian Men Talk about Health, Tobacco and Alcohol*. Aldershot: Avebury.

New York Daily News (2012) www.nydailynews.com/news/national/american-airlines-flight-delayed-attendant-rants-crashing-sept-11-terrorist-attacks-article-1. 1036726 (accessed 15/7/2015).

Nixon, D. (2009) 'I can't put a smiley face on': Working-class masculinity, emotional labour and service work in the 'new economy'. *Gender, Work and Organisation* 16(3): 300–322.

Nowotny, H. (1981) Women in public life in Austria. In C. Fuchs Epstein and R. Laub Coser (eds), *Access to Power: Cross-National Studies of Women and Elites*. London: George Allen & Unwin.

Obholzer, A. (2005) The impact of agency and setting. *Journal of Health Organization and Management* 19(4–5): 297–303.

O'Brien, M. (2008) Gendered capital: Emotional capital and mothers' care work in education. *British Journal of Sociology of Education* 29(2): 137–148.

Ogbonna, E., & Harris, L. C. (2004) Work intensification and emotional labour among UK university lecturers: An exploratory study. *Organization Studies* 25(7): 1185–1203.

Pelzer, P. (2005) The hostility triad: The contribution of negative emotions to organizational (un-) wellness. *Culture and Organization* 11(2): 111–123.

Penn Behavioural Health (2008) Dealing with emotions at work: Ways to reduce conflict and control emotion for more effective workplace interactions. www.pennbehavioralhealth.org/documents/dealing_with_emotions_at_work.pdf (accessed 27/1/2015).

Phillips, M. (2015) Re-ethicizing corporate greening: Ecofeminism, activism and ethics of care. In A. Pullen and C. Rhodes (eds), *The Routledge Companion to Ethics, Politics and Organizations*. London: Routledge.

Probyn, E. (2004) Shame in the habitus. *Sociological Review* 52(s2): 224–248.

Pugh, S. D. (2001) "Service with a smile": Emotional contagion in the service encounter. *Academy of Management Journal* 44(5): 1018–1027.

Pullen, A., & Rhodes, C. (2014) Ethics, embodiment and organizations. *Organization* 22 (2): 159–165.

Pullen, A., & Rhodes, C. (2015) Introduction: The inseparability of ethics and politics in organizations. In A. Pullen and C. Rhodes (eds), *The Routledge Companion to Ethics, Politics and Organizations*. London: Routledge.

Rafaeli, A., & Sutton, R. I. (1987) Expression of emotion as part of the work role. *Academy of Management Review* 12(1): 23–37.

Rafaeli, A., & Sutton, R. (1991) Emotional contrast strategies as means of social influence: Lessons from criminal interrogators and bill collectors. *Academy of Management Journal* 34(4): 749–775.

Raz, A. E. (2002) *Emotions at Work, Normative Control, Organizations and Culture in Japan and America*. Cambridge, MA: Harvard University Press.

Reay, D. (2000) A useful extension of Bourdieu's conceptual framework? Emotional capital as a wat of understanding mother' involvement in their children's education? *Sociological Review* 48(4): 568–585.

Reay, D. (2004) Gendering Bourdieu's concepts of capitals? Emotional capital, women and social class. *Sociological Review* 52(s2): 57–74.

Rein, G., McCraty, R., & Atkinson, M. (1995) The physiological and psychological effects of compassion and anger. *Journal of Advanced Medicine* 8(2): 87–105.

Rhodes, C. (2012) Ethics, alterity and the relationality of leadership justice. *Human Relations* 65(10): 1311–1331.

Roper, M. (1994) *Masculinity and the British Organisation Man since 1945*. Oxon: Oxford University Press.

Rynes, S., Bartunek, J., Dutton, J., & Margolis, J. (2012) Care and compassion through an organizational lens: Opening up new possibilities. *Academy of Management Review* 37(4): 503–523.

Salovey, P., & Mayer, J. (1990) Emotional intelligence. *Imagination, Cognition, and Personality* 9: 185–211.

Sanders, T. (2004) Controllable laughter: Managing sex work through humour. *Sociology* 38(2): 273–291.

Sanders, C. R. (2010) Working out back: The veterinary technician and 'dirty work'. *Journal of Contemporary Ethnography* 39(3): 243–272.

Schnurr, S., & Chan, A. (2011) When laughter is not enough: Responding to teasing and self-denigrating humour at work. *Journal of Pragmatics* 43(1): 20–35.

Scott, B. A., & Barnes, C. M. (2011) A multilevel field investigation of emotional labor, affect, work withdrawal, and gender. *Academy of Management Journal* 54(1): 116–136.

Selmi, G. (2012) Dirty talks and gender cleanliness: An account of identity management practices in phone sex work. In R. Simpson, N. Slutskaya, P. Lewis and H. Hopfl (eds), *Dirty Work Concepts and Identities*. Basingstoke: Palgrave Macmillan.

Sharma, U., & Black, P. (2001) Look good, feel better: Beauty therapy as emotional labour. *Sociology* 35(4): 913–931.

Sharpe, E. K. (2005) 'Going above and beyond': The emotional labour of adventure guides. *Journal of Leisure Research* 37(1): 29–50.

Shuler, S., & Sypher, B. D. (2000) Seeking emotional labour: When managing the heart enhances the work experience. *Management Communication Quarterly* 14(1): 50–89.

Simpson, R., Slutskaya, N., & Hughes, J. (2011) Emotional dimensions of dirty work: Men's encounter with taint in the butcher trade. *International Journal of Work Organisation and Emotion* 4(2): 195–212.

Simpson, R., Slutskaya, N., Lewis, P., & Hopfl, H. (2012) Introduction to R. Simpson, N. Slutskaya, P. Lewis and H. Hopfl (eds), *Dirty Work Concepts and Identities*. Basingstoke: Palgrave Macmillan.

Six Feet Under (2001–2005) HBO. Created by Alan Ball.

Smith, A. C., & Kleinman, S. (1989) Managing emotions in medical school: Students' contact with the living and the dead. *Social Psychology Quarterly* 52: 56–69.

Stacey, C. (2005) Finding dignity in dirty work: The constraints and rewards of low-wage home care labour. *Sociology of Health & Illness* 27(6): 831–854.

Stanley, L., & MacKenzie-Davey, K. (2012) From high flyer to crook. In R. Simpson, N. Slutskaya, P. Lewis and H. Hopfl (eds), *Dirty Work Concepts and Identities*. Basingstoke: Palgrave Macmillan.

Stannard, C. (1973) Old folks and dirty work: The social conditions for patient abuse in a nursing home. *Social Problems* 20(3): 329–342.

Stearns, P. N., & Stearns, C. Z. (1985) Emotionology: Clarifying the history of emotions and emotional standards. *The American Historical Review* 90(4): 813–836.

Stein, M. (2007) Toxicity and the unconscious experience of the body at the employee-customer interface. *Organization Studies* 28(8): 1223–1241.

Strauss, A (1978) *Negotiations: Varieties, Contexts, Processes and Social Order*. San Francisco: Jossey-Bass.

Sturdy, A., & Fineman, S. (2001) Struggles for the control of affect: Resistance as politics and emotion. In A. Sturdy, I. Grugulis and H. Willmott (eds), *Customer Service: Empowerment and entrapment*. Basingstoke: Palgrave.

Sutton, R. (1991) Maintaining norms about expressed emotions: The case of bill collectors. *Administrative Science Quarterly* 36: 245–268.

Taylor, S. (1998) Emotional labour and the new workplace. In P. Thompson and C. Wharhurst (eds), *Workplaces of the Future*. London: Macmillan.

Taylor, S., & Tyler, M. (2000) Emotional labour and sexual difference in the airline industry. *Work, Employment & Society* 14(1): 77–95.

Terkel, S. (1974) *Working*. London: The New Press.

Thoits, P. (1985) Self-labelling processes in mental illness: The role of emotional deviance. *American Journal of Sociology* 91: 221–249.

Thompson, W. E. (1991) Handling the stigma of the dead: Morticians and funeral directors. *Deviant Behaviour* 12(4): 403–429.

Tijsterman, S., & Overeem, P. (2008) Escaping the iron cage: Weber and Hegel on bureaucracy and freedom. *Administrative Theory and Practice* 30(1): 71–91.

Tracy, S. J. (2000) Becoming a character for commerce: Emotional labour, self-subordination, and discursive construction of identity in a total institution. *Management Communication Quarterly* 14(1): 90–128.

Tracy, S. J. (2005) Locking up emotion: Moving beyond dissonance for understanding emotion labour discomfort. *Communication Monographs* 72(3): 261–283.

Tracy, S. J., & Scott, C. (2006) Sexuality, masculinity, and taint management among firefighters and correctional officers. *Management Communication Quarterly* 20(1): 6–38.

Tyler, M. (2012) Glamour girls, macho men and everything in between: Un/doing gender and dirty work in Soho's sex shops. In R. Simpson, N. Slutskaya, P. Lewis and H. Hopfl (eds), *Dirty Work Concepts and Identities*. Basingstoke: Palgrave Macmillan.

Tyler, M., & Taylor, S. (2001) Juggling Justice and Care: Gendered Customer Service in the Contemporary Airline Industry. In A. Sturdy, I. Grugulis and H. Willmott (eds), *Customer Service: Empowerment and Entrapment*. London: Palgrave.

Van Dijk, P. A., & Kirk Brown, A. (2006) Emotional labour and negative job outcomes: An evaluation of the mediating role of dissonance. *Journal of Management and Organization* 12: 101–115.

Van Maanen, J. (1978) The asshole. In P. Manning and J. Van Maanen (eds), *Policing: A view from the Street*. Culver City: Goodyear.

Van Maanen, J. (1991) The smile factory: Work at Disneyland. In P. J. Frost (ed.), *Reframing Organisational Culture*. London: Sage.

Vaughan, D. (1999) The dark side of organizations: Mistake, misconduct, and disaster. *Annual Review of Sociology* 25: 271–305.

Vey, M. (2005) Avoiding the dark side of service with a smile. Accenture Research Note. www.researchgate.net/researcher/2015300234_Meredith_A_Vey (accessed 23/4/2015).

Voronov, M., & Vince, R. (2012) Integrating emotions into the analysis of institutional work. *Academy of Management Review* 37(1): 58–81.

Waddington, K. (2012) *Gossip and Organizations*. London: Routledge.

Ward, J., & McMurray, R. (2011) The unspoken work of general practitioner receptionists: A re-examination of emotion management in primary care. *Social Science & Medicine* 72(10): 1583–1587.

Warner, M. (2007) Karka, Weber and organization theory. *Human Relations* 60(7): 1019–1038.

Webb, J., Schirato, T., & Danaher, G. (2013) *Understanding Bourdieu*. London: Sage.

Weber, M. (1946) *Essays in Sociology*. New York: Oxford University Press.

Weber, M. (1978) *Economy and Society: An Outline of Interpretive Sociology*. Berkeley: University of California Press.

Wharton, A. S. (2009) The sociology of emotional labour. *Annual Review of Sociology* 35: 147–165.

Williams, C. (2003) Sky service: The demands of emotional labour in the airline industry. *Gender, Work and Organization* 10: 513–550.

Willmott, H. (1993) Strength is ignorance; slavery is freedom: Managing culture in modern organizations. *Journal of Management Studies* 30: 515–553.

Wouters, C. (1989a) The sociology of emotions and flight attendants: Hochschild's managed heart. *Theory, Culture & Society* 6: 95–123.

Wouters, C. (1989b) Response to Hochschild's reply. *Theory, Culture & Society* 6: 447–450.

Zapf, D. (2002) Emotion work and psychological well-being: A review of the literature and some conceptual considerations. *Human Resource Management Review* 12: 237–268.

Zembylas, M. (2007) Emotional capital and education: Theoretical insights from Bourdieu. *British Journal of Education Studies* 55(1): 443–463.

Index

toxin handlers 13

veterinarians 2, 13, 49, 50, 57, 69, 71, 90, 102–3; veterinary surgeons 11, 14, 96
volunteers 47, 79, 80, 84, 85, 99, 120

waiters 2, 46
Weber, Max 36, 37
women 3, 5, 8, 12, 16, 32, 60, 64, 98, 119; gendered accounts and 8
work: emotional support 85; low-skilled 9; social control 27; tainted 59, 63, 66, 71

For Product Safety Concerns and Information please contact our EU
representative GPSR@taylorandfrancis.com
Taylor & Francis Verlag GmbH, Kaufingerstraße 24, 80331 München, Germany